GUIDE TO
COIN
COLLECTING

PATTERN COINS

GUIDE TO
COIN
COLLECTING

BY DAVID L. GANZ

Collins
An Imprint of HarperCollinsPublishers

*To Elvira ("Lisa") Clain-Stefanelli and Vladimir ("Doc") Clain-Stefanelli
and the national numismatic collection that they helped to build and modernize,*

and

*For Kathy, my wife, who is not a coin collector but shares with me my passion for a fascinating hobby that I
have written about, and pursued, for five decades.*

HarperCollins books may be purchased for educational, business, or sales promotional use. For information please write: Special Markets Department, HarperCollins Publishers, 10 East 53rd Street, New York, NY 10022.

FIRST EDITION

The name of the "Smithsonian," "Smithsonian Institution," and the sunburst logo are registered trademarks of the Smithsonian Institution.

Produced by BAND-F Ltd, www.band-f.com
President / Partner: f-stop fitzgerald
Director of Development: Karen Jones
Production Editor: Mie Kingsley
Production Manager and Interior Design: Maria Fernandez
Digital Art Technician: Weston Minissali

Library of Congress Cataloging-in-Publication Data

Ganz, David L.
  Guide to coin collecting / by David L. Ganz. — 1st ed.
     p. cm.
  Includes bibliographical references.
  ISBN 978-0-06-134140-3
  1. Coins—Collectors and collecting—Handbooks, manuals, etc. 2.
Coins, American—Collectors and collecting—Handbooks, manuals, etc. I.
Title.

  CJ81.G36 2008
  737.4--dc22

2007027768

08 09 10 11 12   TOP   10 9 8 7 6 5 4 3 2 1

CONTENTS

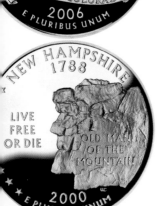

INTRODUCTION

An Endless Fascination

The United States Mint estimates that one in three Americans—some 139 million people—collect coins.

Why is that?

People collect objects of all kinds for a variety of reasons, but there are common factors that explain why people collect coins, and even choose to become serious collectors (known as "numismatists").

Coins are a common part of our everyday life; we see them countless times a day as we use pocket change for buying and selling. We might notice an older coin in circulation and wonder why it remains available, or through whose hands it may have passed. Some of them we put aside and save. Perhaps this ignites our collecting passion.

If we see an older coin at a flea market, in a hobby shop, or elsewhere, we may even wonder why we would pay more than face value for it. Then we turn on the television or radio news and hear the story of a $20 gold piece from 1933 that sold for millions of dollars—or that a coin that appears to have been imprinted twice is worth many times its face value.

Most likely we collect coins because we are fascinated: with history, politics, military success, sociology, intellectual pursuits, or with the development of Western civilization. Or because we

America's rarest coin, the 1933 double eagle or $20 gold piece, was designed by renowned sculptor Augustus Saint-Gaudens at the request of president Theodore Roosevelt. Augustus Saint-Gaudens designed the obverse and reverse of the $20 gold piece issued 1907–1933. The coin contains .9675 troy ounces of gold.

look at coinage as miniaturized art with themes we want to collect such as animals, ships, cars, or historical objects.

We see America's heroes depicted on its coinage: George Washington, Abraham Lincoln, Thomas Jefferson, Franklin Delano Roosevelt, and John F. Kennedy. Advertising for the U.S. Mint's commemorative coin products appeals simultaneously to our sentimentality and to our avarice. Daily newspapers report on the price of metals used in coins and on the threat that rising copper and zinc prices have posed to the survival of the penny and the nickel.

So yes, coins are fascinating. *The Guide to Coin Collecting* explores the story of how coins came about, and how and why we collect them. We will look at what there is to collect, and the fun that comes from both discovering the amazing diversity of coin designs, and from watching your collection grow.

America's heroes on a modern proof set. Presidential portraits began with Lincoln in 1909 and have been steadily added ever since.

The Hobby of Kings—and Elephants, Too

What do Roman emperor Caesar Augustus; France's great Sun King, Louis XIV; King Farouk of Egypt; the Duke of Windsor (King Edward VIII); and King Victor Emmanuel II of Italy all have in common? They were coin collectors. This is why coin collecting is called the king of hobbies, and the hobby of kings.

Coin collecting has existed almost from the time that coinage was invented—around 750 B.C. by the Lydians—though it was not until several centuries later that the Roman Emperor Caesar Augustus took collecting to a new level by keeping a collection of coins from throughout the known world. In ancient times, coins were the newspapers of the day. Coin designs celebrated major military victories, and coin inscriptions described the battles. One of the earliest known portraits of Jesus—and the basis for subsequent depictions of him—comes from eighth-century Byzantine coinage. Money is a window into politics, a spotlight on history's winners and losers.

Coins were initially intended for circulation and use; later, collectors—mostly nobility—began to acquire coins for their beauty and historical significance. During the Renaissance, people other than nobles began to collect money from around the world, and exquisite medallion coins were created for sheer artistic value. Coin collections were founded that today are exhibited in world-class museums: The royal coin collections of Sweden and Denmark, the collection of the Vatican Museum, and the national collections of the Banco de Mexico and Bank of Ecuador are well known. Even the French storybook character Babar the Elephant has a royal coin collection.

America's Coin Collection Begins

The Smithsonian Institution has been America's preeminent numismatic showcase for nearly a century and it is one of the world's greatest collections, public or private. But at first, the Smithsonian's collection of coins was virtually nonexistent. The last will and testament of James Smithson, the Scottish immigrant for whom the Smithsonian is named, left money to found the Institution. This grand concept, however, had little follow-through: Although Smithson left gold coins (two of which are still a part of the national numismatic collection) for the bequest, no plan was specified for what the Institution should contain.

Justinian II is depicted on this gold solidus. The coin was struck over 1,300 years ago in what is today modern Turkey.

The nation's first silver dollar, dated 1794, features a stark Liberty design (obverse). Only 1,758 coins were struck at the Philadelphia Mint. Note the young nation symbolized by the puny eagle (reverse). Later dated coins shows the eagle flexing its muscle with a very different design.

The starting point for this national collection of numismatic items was actually from the Mint's own cabinet, painstakingly selected by Mint directors and Philadelphia Mint superintendents for generations. But it is the additional acquisitions and donations that make the collection truly great.

Coins that have found their way into the historic collection range from a unique 1794 silver dollar pattern in copper (donated by Stack's, the New York coin auctioneers), to significant portions of the Chase Manhattan Bank Money Museum. The bulk of the Chase collection—including a famous 1804 silver dollar—went to the Smithsonian around 1978.

The cornerstone of the Smithsonian's current million-object coin collection consists of the former holdings of Josiah K. Lilly, the scion of the pharmaceutical company, whose 6,500 gold coins include virtually every major rarity in the world in superior states of preservation, every one a quality museum piece.

Quietly and anonymously, Lilly had been a client of Stack's for many years. When he died, his heirs offered his fabulous collection to the Smithsonian in exchange for a credit against the tax due on the estate. It took an act of Congress, but the collection was handed over for continuing display.

Mint records say 19,000 silver dollars were made in 1804. None were. This type I coin (39-40 mm) was made at the Mint circa 1858 (and dated 1804). Reverse of type I 1804 silver dollar. Note the eagle's beak points toward arrows of war, not the olive branch of peace.

A second cornerstone comes from the generosity of collector Paul A. Straub. During the late 1940s and the 1950s (ending with his death in 1958), he donated 1,793 gold coins and 3,855 silver coins from all over the world.

Celebrity Collectors: Coins as Film Stars

Numismatics—the systematic organizing and collecting of coins, tokens, medals, and paper money—was the hobby of American leaders such as Francis Cardinal Spellman and industrialist J. P. Morgan. American presidents John Adams and his son John Quincy Adams were both serious coin collectors, fueled by their diplomatic travels following the American Revolution. Ulysses S. Grant acquired a magnificent collection of Japanese coins in his post-presidential travels. Though better known as a philatelist, or stamp collector, President Franklin Delano Roosevelt was also a coin collector, as well as an avid currency designer; remnants of his designs are still on display at the FDR Presidential Library at Hyde Park, New York.

Super sports agent Dwight Manley, Los Angeles Lakers owner Dr. Jerry Buss, U.S. Senator Mark O. Hatfield (R-Oregon), and Congressman Jimmy Hayes (D-Louisiana) also share a love of coins. Most have been members of the national coin club, the American Numismatic Association.

Coin collecting has also attracted entertainers. Actor Buddy Ebsen, comedian and radio performer Harry ("Parkyakarkas") Einstein, screen star Adolphe Menjou, composer Hoagy Carmichael, musician Benny Goodman, actor and voice personality James Earl Jones, actress-director Penny Marshall, and actor and comedic genius Bill Cosby have all collected coins.

Hollywood has turned coins and coin collecting into an important part of movies and television shows. In 1947, mystery writer Raymond Chandler's *Brasher Doubloon* came to the silver screen, depicting the theft of the rare coin by that name in a Philip Marlowe motion picture starring George Montgomery. A 1964 episode of *The Lucy Show* depicts a character, Jerry, who finds a penny worth 50 cents. Lucy and her sidekick, Viv, withdraw 2,000 pennies

The Brasher Doubloon is the stuff of movies and legend. The minter, Ephraim Brasher, lived on Cherry Street in New York, down the block from President Washington.

Actor Victor Buono "stole" the world's most valuable coin, a 1913 Liberty nickel, on the *Hawaii Five-O* television show in 1973.

from the bank, and search through them until they find one worth $16.50.

A 1964 *Perry Mason* episode entitled "Wooden Nickels" involved Raymond Burr in a case featuring a Confederate half dollar alleged to be worth $50,000, and a 1913 Liberty-head nickel whose value is specified in the script at $22,000. In a 1973 *Hawaii Five-0* episode, "The $100,000 Nickel," Victor Buono plays a villain who steals the world's most valuable coin, another 1913 Liberty nickel. Two movies with similar names—1989's *See No Evil, Hear No Evil*, a comedy starring Richard Pryor and Gene Wilder, and 1993's *Hear No Evil*, starring Marlee Matlin and Martin Sheen—also used valuable stolen coins as the underlying plot device. The popular twenty-first century television series *CSI* even has a leading character who is depicted as a coin collector.

History Motivates Collecting

The largest growth spurt in contemporary numismatics in the United States took place in the quarter century following the end of the Second World War.

Several events conspired to help coin collecting come of age in the twentieth century. In 1909, the Lincoln cent was created as a circulating commemorative coin recalling the centennial of the birth of Abraham Lincoln. Shortly before the penny's introduction, Augustus Saint-Gaudens and Bella Lyon Pratt, sculptors of international renown, redesigned the eagle quarter, $5 gold piece, $10 eagle coin, and $20 double eagle coin. Then came the 1913 buffalo, or Indian head, nickel design revision by James Earle Fraser, followed in 1916 by the design revisions on the dime and half dollar (Adolph A. Weinman), quarter (Hermon McNeil), and the issuance of a peace dollar (Anthony DeFrancisci) in 1921. This combined face change in American coinage brought out the collecting instinct in a vast number of citizens.

The second motivating factor occurred during the Great Depression. The driving engine of the international economy at that time was gold, and all citizens had the right to own gold, which they did in the form of circulating gold coins. Terrified because of the struggling economy, people began to hoard the gold coins.

Gold reserves diminished as the Depression worsened. Shortly after Franklin Delano Roosevelt took office on March 4, 1933, he issued a presidential proclamation ordering millions of dollars' worth of gold coinage turned in to the government. Only rare and unusual gold coins were exempt—enough to allow coin collectors to maintain collections.

Over the previous century, 351 million gold coins, worth $4.5 billion, had been struck. Most were produced with gold valued at $20.67 an ounce. The new price amounted to a devaluation of the dollar—nearly a 70 percent change. Collectors benefited: the gold coins provided a hedge against inflation and against further depreciation of the dollar.

The third significant factor in the development of coin collecting was the 1960 discovery, in someone's pocket change, of a mint error in the small date and the large date versions of the cent. Though the mutant penny did not have substantial value, it focused attention on pocket change that, coupled with an emerging coin shortage, kept the mainstream press focused on coinage and coin collecting.

Then in 1965, there was a changeover to clad coinage—a sandwich of copper core and nickel outside. This attracted a new generation of coin collectors and also made available an entirely new series of coins to collect.

A final factor that has recast coin collecting is the state quarter program, begun in 1999 and continuing until 2008 when all fifty states will have been represented. The success of the state quarter program led to the 2004–2005 Lewis & Clark nickels, the presidential dollar and first ladies' gold coinage starting in 2007, and many other new collectibles.

No wonder, then, that coin collecting is so popular! Coins are history. They are art. They are geography. They depict our cultural icons. Our coins are a mirror of who we are . . . a lasting snapshot of history that you can hold in your hand.

State quarters were made from 1999 to 2008 for each of 50 States. Production of these coins has returned $5 billion in seigniorage to the American taxpayer.

CHAPTER ONE

THE HISTORY
OF COINAGE

Coinage: A Quick World Tour

Before coins were invented, various items were used as currency: wampum, cowrie shells, cat-eye peas, arrowheads. Five thousand years ago in Babylonia and Sumeria, clay tablets were even employed as a kind of IOU.

Coinage began some 2,800 years ago in the kingdom of Lydia, located in modern-day Turkey. In Lydia, coins were made of electrum, a natural gold-and-silver alloy, whose composition was between 40 and 55 percent gold and the rest silver, usually with trace elements of copper. Electrum was melted, shaped, and punched with primitive die markings.

From the electrum coins used in Lydia in 750 B.C., to spade money used in China as early as 600 B.C., to silver ingots and measures of gold—all are part of the history of money. Other units of exchange included the livestock standard of ancient Persia and the Mongols; the cattle standard of Colombia; the cocoa bean of Mexico; and "knife money" used in many countries. Traditionally, numismatists have referred to these rare (and therefore collectible) surviving examples of early currency as "primitive" or "odd and curious" money.

OPPOSITE: The trade dollar.

Electrum, a low-grade gold, was used to produce coins in Lydia (modern-day Turkey) circa 750 B.C.

The world's first coinage was struck in Lydia. Many examples were dug up during the Marshall Plan reconstruction in the late 1940s.

"Primitive" money was odd in the sense that it was not legal tender, but was widely used at more-or-less agreed-upon values. Each item was unique, which adds to the collectible attraction; for example, polished wampum was beautiful,

China used "spade money," so-called for its shape, as early as 600 B.C. Unlike traditional coins, these are cast from molten metal, not struck.

colorful and distinctive, and no two pieces were quite the same.

Economic functionality was the basis of primitive money, which is why livestock standards were so successful. In Kenya, for example, goats and cattle were still widely used on the eve of World War II. Paul Einzig, in the book *Primitive Money*, describes goats as "small change," while cattle were worth more; a longer explanation appeared in *Facing Mount Kenya*, written in 1938 by a graduate student of the London School of Economics named Jomo Kenyatta—who later went on to lead Kenya to independence and modernity. (Interestingly, even this primitive system suffered from inflation: During the First World War, the dowry bride price was 70 goats. By 1935, Einzig quotes a price of 90 goats!)

China was the first to experiment with paper money around the beginning of the ninth century A.D.; its silk notes circulated as far away as Europe. Coins of the ancient Greeks also circulated widely.

Seleucus, Wise Old King of the Ancient World

Seleucus Nicator was probably the second most powerful man in the ancient world next to his mentor Alexander the Great. Historians today credit Seleucus with extending Hellenistic influence over Syria, Iran, and the Middle East. By 312 B.C., Seleucus took firm control over Babylon, and that same year marked the beginning of the Seleucid dynasty, which lasted until around the year 67 B.C., when Pompey crushed its forces in the name of the Roman Empire.

Seleucus' victory of Ipsos over Antigonos in 301 B.C. solidified his rule over a large swath of Asia and the Middle East.

Coinage of Seleucus I was struck at several different minting facilities in Asia Minor. Silver tetradrachms were produced at Sardes. Struck sometime between 282 and 281 B.C., the convex obverse depicts the head of young Heracles, facing right, in lionskin battle helmet. Complementing the cheekpiece on the helmet is a bull's horn and ear.

Another coin, found by the late U.S. State Department official Robert F. Kelley, depicts Seleucus regaled in splendor. This coin is now in the collection of the American Numismatic Society in New York City. On the reverse is Nike, the Greek goddess of victory, depicted crowning a trophy of armaments.

Seleucus, building his dynasty to the end, decided to move on to Macedonia, to complete the empire that Alexander had intended. But for a man of seventy-eight, it was simply too much; he was murdered en route to the land where he was born.

But even as the Chinese were casting their knife and spade monies and the Lydians were producing the first die-struck coins, the rest of the world used more primitive forms of money. During the time of the Romans, salt remained a major method of payment to the legions (soldiers), even though the empire had established branch mints throughout the provinces. Barter was also widely used.

Today, the magnificent Shanghai Museum has an outstanding display of its special permanent coin exhibit. This exhibit traces Chinese money from the Shang dynasty (sixteenth century B.C.) to

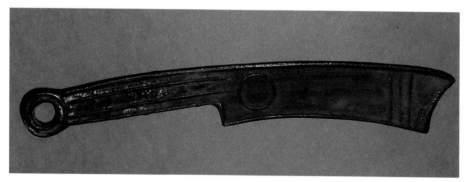

So-called knife money from China, used 450–250 B.C. Like spade money, it was cast rather than struck and acquires a patina with age.

Gold stater from the mid 1st century B.C. featuring a Roman consul walking left, accompanied by two lictors (guards) and an eagle standing on a scepter.

the Zhou Dynasty (until about 770 B.C.), through the Qin dynasty (circa 221 B.C.) and the Yuan, Ming, and Qing dynasties (A.D. 1279–1911).

On display are real and bronze cowrie shells; metal weights that were smelted (without denomination), including gold plates; numerous cast coins; and molds for making coins. Spade coins—shaped like a shovel, with a hollow handle and pointed tips—abound in the display. There are also sword coins or knife money, with rings at the end of the handle both to string the coins together and for convenience in counting.

There are examples of so-called "key money," coinage from the Xin Mang government (A.D. 9–23), which replaced the five-zhu coin from the Than Dynasty. Cast coins, with round and square holes, complete the offering of ancient Chinese coins. In some cases, the museum has the original coin molds that came from the first casts.

The coinage of the Hellenistic world—the money of ancient Greece—depicted in beautifully engraved die work the buildings of the era and the gods that they honored. The beauty of Greek coins rivals that of ancient Rome and of the Byzantine emperors at Constantinople.

The Smithsonian's National

Tetradrachm from Athens featuring the head of Athena wearing a crested helmet. The owl on the reverse was also a symbol for Athena.

A gold sultani, the first gold coin struck by the Ottomans in occupied Greece.

Numismatic Collection (NNC) has an extraordinary sampling of ancient coins. A magnificent group comes from the collection of Josiah K. Lilly, including thirty-eight ancient Greek gold coins, sixty gold aurei of Roman emperors, and seventeen Byzantine gold coins. Eventually, through economic evolution and monetary revolution, coins and currency became the primary instrument of commerce. Of course, by the early twenty-first century, credit and debit cards, checks, and other ways of recording transactions made "hard money" a relative term.

Early Coin Production Methods

Manufacturing of ancient coinage was truly an art. In some respects it was similar to the process still used today, but in other respects much more simplistic. In the twenty-first century, mints strike coins on presses capable of manufacturing 600 coins per minute, producing substantially identical coins from many different dies. More than 100,000 models of a coin are produced from each die before it wears out; at peak production, the die shop of the U.S. Mint of Philadelphia operates twenty-four hours a day, seven days a week. By comparison, ancient coins were produced one at a time, in a labor-intensive minting process.

In ancient times, even more important than the artistry of the design was the coin-manufacturing method, from which today's production techniques derive. The process of using a die was pretty much the same for Greek coinage of 600 B.C. as for its descendants 2,600 years later: an engraver takes a flat piece of metal and cuts, in reverse, the image that will rise from the planchet, or **flan**, as the blank metal is called. The heated planchet is pressed between the top and bottom parts of the die; pressure on the mold (usually struck upon an anvil) causes the compressed metal to flow into the mold and form the design. Today, mechanical devices replace handwork, but the production process remains the same.

A Sicilian tetradrachm, circa 415-405 B.C. showing a charioteer with Nike flying above. The die was signed by the engraver, Eumenes, whose initials EV can be seen.

The deeper the engraver cuts into the steel (the **negative image**), the higher the relief, or contrast, on the coin (the **positive image**) when it is removed from the die. The shallower the engraving in the die, the lower the relief. For a portrait, the nose would be the high (or low) point, the forehead and chin less prominent.

Blanks were hand-cut and carved to the right size and weight, then heated, or **annealed**, in fires or ovens to soften them. They were then placed between the **obverse** (top) die and the **reverse** (bottom) die; hammering the die then pushed the die into the softened metal and vice versa. The metal naturally spread along the path of least resistance, into the mold cavity of the die, to create the coin. If the coin was over the desired weight it could be trimmed; if underweight, it was usually melted and cast all over again. As you can see, minting in the old days was an extremely physical and labor-intensive means of production.

The method invented by the Lydians and the Greeks was essentially the one used more than 1,600 years later in the Renaissance, when artist and inventor Leonardo da Vinci sketched plans for a coining press designed to speed production. In the late twentieth century, International Business Machines (IBM) took the da Vinci notebooks and produced a replica of his minting machine that they found would indeed work— striking, coining, and cutting planchets simultaneously.

In the 1550s, screw-press technology, invented by German silversmith Marx Schwab,

replaced hand-production coinage. Heavy, iron-leveraged screws pressed the coin metal to the desired thickness.

Three centuries passed before the next innovation arrived: in 1838, steam coinage presses were implemented. Dies were still being cut by hand, but beginning some thirty years later, the Hill and the Janvier reduction engraving machines offered a method of copying designs onto coin dies similar to the pantograph used in other fields.

What's on a Coin?

Up until the time of Caesar, Roman coins avoided human deification. A silver denarius glorifying Caesar's victory over Pompey showed an elephant trampling a snake.

Historian Carroll Quigley postulated that coins in ancient times, particularly in Rome, were virtually the newspapers of the day. Important battles won and lost were commemorated on coinage;

Silver Denarius: Caesar's victory over Pompey. The elephant, symbolizing Julius Caesar, presaged the use of imperial portraiture.

A gold solidus featuring Justinian I of Constantinople. Robert F. Kelley was a diplomat who served in Turkey administering the Marshall Plan. He bought many ancient coins during his stay and later donated them to the ANS.

likewise, Brutus's murder of Caesar on the Ides of March was an image on a widely circulated coin.

The artisans who became coin engravers were the equivalent of the celebrity photographers of today. The images in our minds of what Caesar or Nero looked like, and how various buildings were constructed, come largely from ancient Greek and Roman coin design.

A gold solidus of Justinian II made around A.D. 695 bears the earliest known coinage portrait of Jesus. There are many versions of this image because of the number of hand-cut dies; one example appears in the Robert F. Kelley collection

A gold aureus decorated with the profile of Nero.

housed in the Museum of the American Numismatic Society in New York City.

The artistry of coin images from the Greek, Roman, and Byzantine empires is obvious today. But the art of coin portraiture disappeared in the Dark Ages (roughly from A.D. 476 to A.D. 1000) and Middle Ages, as if the artistry and production techniques were simply forgotten.

Coinage of the Middle Ages (approximately A.D. 800 to 1400) was mostly primitive in design, composition, refinement, and minting technique. The feudal economy had little use for money, anyway, as the barter system of pre-Greco-Roman times returned to the forefront. For the most part, coinage designs of the Dark and Middle Ages are not particularly interesting, but they do have historic significance. They also document loss of culture, art, and even the rudiments of a modern economy.

During the Dark Ages in Europe, the coin stamper had to be very careful: if a coin was lost or

Coinage of the Visigoths. The coinage is primitive, and not widely collected, but is an important accompaniment to the Dark Ages in Europe.

Coinage of Egyptian Ptolemies

The first regular coinage in Egyptian antiquity was that of the Ptolemies, who came to prominence following the death of Alexander the Great. Both Ptolemy I Soter and his successor, Ptolemy II Philadelphus, were devoted to the developments of the arts and sciences. During their reigns, museums and research laboratories flourished. Ptolemy I, intent upon making Alexandria an economic as well as cultural rival of Athens, developed a new, lighter-weight standard for coinage which helped to establish a self-sufficient Egyptian economy.

Of particular interest is a gold coin known as the Adelphon-Theon, which depicts the first two generations of Ptolemies. The Adelphon-Theon gold piece measures approximately 28 millimeters in diameter and weighs 428 grains. Also known as a "mnaieia," the gold coin of this series equaled 100 drachms, or one mina, of silver.

The reverse of the coin presents busts of Ptolemy I Soter and his wife Berenice enclosed in a circumference of raised dots. Both busts, which face right, are cloaked and crowned with diadems; Ptolemy wears a chalmys, or fine woolen mantel, and Berenice wears a veil. In Egyptian fashion, the rulers became divine after death, thus the word "Theon" appears above the heads of these two, indicating their deification by the Egyptian people.

The obverse of the coin also depicts two busts in a ring of raised dots, but these portraits are captured with the word "Adelphon," meaning "two from the same stem": Ptolemy II Philadelphus and his wife Arsinoe II are each the son and daughter of Ptolemy I and Berenice. This was the first instance of the Greek kings of Egypt marrying their sisters.

Once again, the pair faces right and is diademed; Ptolemy II wears a chalmys, and Arsinoe II a veil. To the left of these busts is an oval shield.

The "Adelphon" face of the coin is significant because of the rare rendering of Ptolemy II. Arsinoe II, the stronger and more vibrant of the two, was instantly proclaimed a goddess upon her death in 270 B.C., and appears alone on gold coins of several denominations. The face of Ptolemy II has proved more elusive.

Due to the tremendous number of "Adelphon-Theon" coins which were minted, both as mnaieion and as a half-piece, the coin holds a place of great importance in both the history of Ptolemaic currency and the mysterious land of Egypt.

stolen, the guilty party's hand was cut off and nailed to the workshop door.

The Goths, or Vandals, and the Lombards imitated the Roman monetary system as well as the iconography of its coinage. Vandal kings issued imitation Roman gold solidi with their own portraits, and placed their names on coins made of bronze and silver.

The coinage of the Byzantine Empire continued for nearly a thousand years. Emperor Alexius I Comnenus (1081–1118) defended Byzantium from the Turks, and financed his effort by melting down public monuments to make bronze coinage. But most of the Byzantine coinage was gold, much of which was used to pay the salaries of mercenary troops. Unlike coins of earlier times, these coins were not flat but cup-shaped, with the concave face bearing the imperial portrait. The Virgin Mary appears on many of the coins, though Saint George, Saint Theodore, or Saint Demetrius sometimes took her place.

The political and economic stability of the

European Middle Ages led to many new nation-states that promptly exercised their rights of sovereignty by issuing coins, especially as the Middle Ages gave way to the early Renaissance and the rediscovery of numismatic arts. A thirst for travel and to expand trade reached Europe after the journeys of Marco Polo. He brought news and customs of the Orient—where paper money circulated in China and strange coins shaped like keys and knives were widespread. On the Grand Canal at Piazza San Marco in Polo's home city of Venice, a mint, or Zecca, soon churned out gold ducats, coins used for trade the world over.

A ducatone struck in Renaissance Italy for Philip II of Spain.

The Mint at Venice today. From this famous site off the Grand Canal in the Piazza San Marco is the Mint that produced ducats that traveled to the orient with Marco Polo and all over the rest of the known world.

The art on Renaissance coins reflected other culture changes. Whatever could be sculpted was also engraved. In some places, coin sizes grew to thirty-five millimeters—almost an inch and a half—and nonmonetary coins, called medals, were produced solely for their artistic merit. Antonio Pisanello (1395–1455) was a master of classical portraiture on the art medal. Eventually, medal portraiture was used on coins of smaller size.

Metals, Moniers, Mints, and Exploration

Silver, the main coining medal of the Middle Ages, was brought into circulation after its discovery in Melle in western France. At almost the same time, Frankish moniers and nobles began to issue their own coinage.

By A.D. 751, coinage resumed under the authority of the crown, and the number of moniers and mints were reduced substantially. Charlemagne (Charles the Great) instituted coinage reform under which twelve deniers equaled one solidus, and twenty solidi equaled one pound of silver bullion. In a published note, Elvira Clain-Stefanelli, while curator of the Smithsonian Institution's National Coin Collection, explained that the identical relationship ratio continued for more than a thousand years until 1967, when Britain finally decimalized its (12) pence = (1) shillings, and 20 shillings = 1 pound (£1) coinage.

As Europe seemingly became smaller, the horizons of numismatics grew with the discovery of a New World: the Western Hemisphere, where Native Americans utilized primitive money—not the coins with which Europeans were familiar—as currency.

The Treaty of Tordesillas in 1492 divided the New World between Portugal and Spain. The Portuguese developed Brazil as the Spanish developed the rest of Latin America, exporting Brazilian escudo coinage back to Europe. Meanwhile, the

A Spanish gold double castellano featuring Fernando V and Isabel I.

defeat of the Moors on the Iberian peninsula meant Spain was unified under Ferdinand and Isabella, a unity that ushered in a whole new era of coinage.

By 1535, Spain's conquest of Mexico was complete, and the first mint in the New World was built in Mexico City. Though the location has changed many times since, the Mexico City Mint is the oldest continually operating facility in the western hemisphere.

The riches of Spain's colonies—precious metals minted into gold and silver coins—were exported back to the mother country. Millions of dollars in silver and lesser—but still impressive—quantities of gold were exported. Struck as "ocho reales," or eight reales ("real" was the currency) and its fractional parts, the coinage was extensive, the values almost unimaginable. Some treasure ships never made it back across the ocean, lost to pirates, privateers, ships of prey, or simply bad weather—the contents seemingly lost for eternity at the bottom of the ocean. In the twentieth century, technology allowed for the rediscovery of these ships, which brought the coinage of the sixteenth century back to the forefront after being untouched, except by seawater, for some 400 years.

The story of *La Galga de Andalucia*—"The Greyhound of Andalucia"—is perhaps typical. A fifty-gun frigate commissioned into the Spanish navy, she sailed for Buenos Aires in 1736 to join squadrons patrolling the Atlantic and Caribbean. For the next fourteen years, *La Galga* served as a convoy escort, traveling mainly between Veracruz, Havana, and Spain's principal home naval base at Cadiz.

Under the command of Don Daniel Houny, an Irishman in the service of Spain, *La Galga* left Havana, Cuba, on its last voyage on August 7, 1750. Charged with escorting a convoy of merchant ships across the Atlantic Ocean to Cadiz, *La Galga* ran into a hurricane near Bermuda. The storm separated the ships in the convoy and forced them westward toward the American coast. During the seven-day storm, *La Galga* lost three masts and began to take on water. Efforts to lighten the ship by pushing her cannon overboard were unsuccessful, and on August 25, she sank off the coast near the Maryland/Virginia border. Most of her crew and passengers were able to reach land safely. Following the wreck, Captain Houny attempted to salvage items from the wreck, but was hindered by local residents' looting. In November, Captain Houny got the help of Governor Ogle of Maryland in protecting the wreck, but before salvage could continue, a second storm came and broke up what was left of the ship.

La Galga lay undisturbed for almost 250 years, until salvage attempts began in the 1980s. In the twenty-first century, a treasure of numismatic riches was extracted. The legal case involving ownership and the issue of whether Spain abandoned the ship and its treasure was still being litigated in the new millennium.

At the height of Spanish power, Spanish mints were set up all over Latin America—all the better to extract mineral treasures, refine them, and send the treasure back to Spain. Virtually all of these coin types are well catalogued and highly collectible today. At the same time, because they were made in quantity, they remain very affordable reminders of the Age of Exploration and its consequences.

CHAPTER TWO

AMERICAN COINAGE HISTORY

Coinage of the Revolution and the States

The money of North America was first produced in Virginia and Massachusetts, though eventually all of what later became the thirteen original colonies created or authorized money. By the early 1650s, handmade dies were used to strike coins in Massachusetts, followed by coinage adorned with a willow tree (starting in 1653), an oak tree (1660) and a pine tree (starting about 1667 but bearing a 1652 date). Maryland and New Jersey also issued coins, as did a number of private minters. However, by the American Revolution a severe coin shortage existed in the colonies. Colonies even started to authorize paper money. At the same time, experimentation with a coined "Continental dollar" took place.

Thomas Jefferson, the third president, and Alexander Hamilton, the first Secretary of the Treasury, wrote extensively about coins, and each played a role in the evolution of the American coinage system. So did Benjamin Franklin—a printer of colonial banknotes—and George Washington, who thought it too royalist to have his portrait placed on coins of the day. (Ironically, Washington today is depicted on the quarter, the dollar bill, and the 2007 presidential

OPPOSITE: 1907 high relief double eagle by Augustus Saint-Gaudens.

This colonial coinage struck circa 1652 is the earliest New England (Massachusetts) coinage. The design was also used on a 3 pence and 6 pence coin, both of which are scarce. The number on the coin tells its value: A Roman numeral for twelve is a shilling under the British system utilized until 1967.

The Pine Tree shilling was struck with a 1652 date from 1667 to 1682 in Massachusetts and achieved respectable circulation. The older date was used under a warrant to produce coins that had been withdrawn by the later date. The Mother Goose nursery rhyme about a "Crooked sixpence" would probably have been a Pine Tree sixpence, similar in design to the larger-denominated shilling. A 3 penny coin was also struck with the 1652 date.

dollar coin. Franklin appeared on the half dollar from 1948 to 1963. Jefferson has appeared on the nickel since 1938, albeit with several different portraits, and on yet another 2007 presidential dollar. Hamilton's portrait is featured on the $10 bill.)

The young country decided to use only gold and silver coins, and copper change, as money. But the system was a disaster—largely because from 1789 until the late 1840s, those precious metals were always in short supply. The lack of coins led private banks to issue their own paper money—"broken

Maryland colonial issues feature the portrait of Cecil, Lord Baltimore, and were produced in four undated denominations: penny, fourpence, sixpence, and shilling. All were struck circa 1659. (obverse and reverse)

bank notes" in today's parlance—which were as unsuccessful as the Continental paper dollars, because there were insufficient funds to back up the paper product. Another weakness: Some of the notes, despite intricate designs and fine engraving, came from fictitious or very poor banks.

Understandably, therefore, the Constitutional Convention was leery of the colonial currency "not worth a Continental" and banned issuance of "money" unless it was made of gold, silver, or copper. Just three years after the Constitution was

There was so much of it that the phrase "not worth a continental" was widely used to describe continental currency and the continental dollar. Eventually, the federal constitution required money to be made of gold and silver.

This continental dollar, struck 1776, probably never circulated. During the Revolutionary War, there was little specie (coin) and the revolutionaries relied on promissory notes and paper currency.

adopted, the Mint Act of 1792 called for gold, silver, and copper coinage.

By the time the California gold rush started around 1848, coins contained their full measure of metal. A $20 gold piece contained $19.99 worth of gold, and a silver dollar had that sum of metal, too. But the economic woes of the American Civil War meant a scarcity of precious metals to finance the struggle. In 1863, when the Union was nearly bankrupt, Treasury Secretary Salmon P. Chase urged the federal government to issue paper money to finance the war. The scheme worked, and Chase's innovation saved the Union—only to be declared unconstitutional, after the emergency was over, by newly appointed Chief Justice of the Supreme Court Salmon P. Chase. (Yes, the same one.)

California's gold rush and the Comstock Lode of silver in Nevada, discovered in the late 1850s, solidified the metal money standard for future gen-

erations of world financiers and strengthened the ancient allure of gold and silver.

The Mint Act of 1792 displayed Alexander Hamilton's broad vision—backed by Jefferson—of how a currency system should be managed. Its effects on monetary history were powerful, as its underlying philosophy was the basis for an 1870 report by deputy controller of the currency, John Jay Knox, resulting in the creation of the Bureau of the Mint in 1873.

The Coinage Act of 1873 became the cornerstone of the Mint's modern legal history. Under the act, gold and silver metal, bullion, foreign coin, or plate could be deposited with the Mint where, for a small fee, the Mint would smelt it down and coin it into national money. Each gold coin had its full weight and measure; that is, a gold eagle had just

This "broken bank note" from Paterson, N.J., had a $9 face value. Currency in oddball denominations like $3, $4, $9, and even $12 bills are widely collected. The bank went out of business over 160 years ago.

Specie was in short supply during the Civil War, causing the introduction of paper currency. Spencer Clark, a clerk in the Treasury department, was in charge of fractional paper currency production. He went too far when he put his own portrait on one of the notes. Today, it is illegal for the portrait of a living person to appear on paper money, although it is perfectly legal on coinage.

Founding of the U.S. Mint

An early priority of our nascent nation was production of federal coinage. State coinage and tokens of the post-colonial period are highly collectible today; many feature portraits of George Washington in an imperial pose. Early federal attempts failed to satisfy the need for specie—circulating coin. Lacking a national mint, Congress was left to contract for coinage from private manufacturers such as James Jarvis, who was authorized by Congress in 1787 to acquire 300 tons of copper to produce what is today called the Fugio cent.

America has long been fascinated with its coinage, and its politicians have long been fascinated with its coinage law. This stems from the original debate over whether the United States should have a mint, or whether its money could be better produced using contract coinage.

When Congress moved the seat of government from Philadelphia to Washington, D.C., in 1800, nearly all government agencies were directed to participate in the move. The Mint was exempted, however, and given a two-year extension.

As the two-year period neared conclusion, another extension was sought—a trend that continued until nearly 1830. Each time, the continued existence of the mint came into question, in part because of the high cost of relatively modest coinage production.

By the mid-1830s the issue was settled, and together with branch mints in Denver, San Francisco, and West Point, the Philadelphia Mint continues to churn out the nation's coinage. The Philadelphia Mint has produced more coins than any other mint in the history of the world.

about $10 worth of gold in it. Silver dollars were similarly regulated, as were coins of lesser value. (The historic problem has always been that precious metal prices are generally unstable without a guardian like the Mint to guarantee a fixed price.)

The Feud over Gold and Silver

Starting around 1867, the effects of the silver discoveries in Nevada began to hit the marketplace; instead of costing one dollar to mint a silver dollar, the cost was more like sixty-seven cents. The government found it impossible to allow unregulated quantities of metal to be converted into coin; allowing people to turn inexpensive silver into dollar coins would ravage the economy. By the time the Coinage Act of 1873 was passed, the value of silver had moved to all-time lows. Although those battling for the silver interests, who called the Coinage Act the "Crime of '73," were a major issue in American politics during the last quarter of the nineteenth century. The "Crime of '73" all but abolished silver as a monetary standard. Even though silver's adherents succeeded in having Congress declare that bimetallism (both a gold and silver standard) was the policy of the United States in 1893, in fact it was not. The Act of 1893 declared the policy, but the Gold Standard Act of 1900, which debased silver completely, acknowledged that the two-metal standard was a sham.

The Gold Standard Act put an end to the national debate over "hard" money and "easy" money that had gone on since the passage of the Coinage Act of 1873. It was a debate that had disastrous economic consequences, and considerable political intrigue.

Not four years earlier, William Jennings Bryan had given an emotional speech—about not crucifying mankind "upon a cross of gold"—as the mainstay of his unsuccessful presidential campaign. The declamation marked a watershed in American politics. With passage of the Gold Standard Act, the nation discarded silver and embraced gold.

Within two generations—by 1933—the nation would discard gold as well, making it illegal for citizens to own gold coin or bullion in any capacity except for rare and unusual gold coins, a condition that would remain in effect until December 31, 1974.

Coin Legislation: Metals

Should the basis for American coinage be gold or silver? This dilemma was as old as the country. Early on, American silver coins were worth more melted than coined. By the turn of the nineteenth century, silver dollar coinage was entirely suspended, not to be restarted until the mid-1830s. With no domestic source of gold (until deposits were discovered decades later in the Carolinas and Georgia), there wasn't much gold coinage, either.

Through the early 1800s, there was a real need for coinage. Congress tried to rectify the problem by regulating the value of foreign coins—from Britain, Portugal and elsewhere—that circulated domestically. But Congress had a hard time getting it right because the bullion market was constantly changing. In 1834, Congress fixed the legal value of foreign silver coins from Mexico, Peru, "Chili," and elsewhere in Central America and reduced the weight of foreign gold coins per dollar, revaluing the U.S. dollar in the process. In 1837, Congress did a better job, setting the value of gold at $20.67 an ounce—a rate that would hold for nearly a century and provide substantial stability for legal tender coinage. (Unlike other nations—whose coinage was periodically removed from circulation or made illegal to own or use—all U.S. coins were legal tender for all debts, public or private, with the notable exceptions of a gold

The coinage of 1837 included a large cent (28-29 mm), two types of half dimes (15.5 mm) (one with a bust visible, the other with Liberty seated), two types of dimes, a bust-style quarter and half dollar (30 mm), but no silver dollar or half cent. There was also a $2.50 and $5 gold coin, but no other gold denominations struck.

recall in the 1930s and several attempts to ban melting.)

Through the California gold rush, the Civil War, the expansion of America, and through World War I and beyond, the price of $20.67 for an ounce of gold held stable. To be sure, there were spikes, such as in 1869 when Jay Gould attempted to corner the gold market. But that overall stability came at a price: The monetary system could not expand easily, and the government had difficulty assisting the economy.

In the twilight of the nineteenth century, after passage of the Coinage Act of 1873, the United States Mint operated its parent facility in Philadelphia, and subsidiary mints at Carson City, Nevada (until 1893), New Orleans (until 1909), and San Francisco (until 1955, resuming operation in the mid-1960s).

Conditions in New Orleans and Carson City were less than desirable from every standpoint. Those who collect coins from these branch mints are familiar with many of the die problems, soft strikes, and generally poor quality of the work of those subsidiary mints, even for circulation issues that were ground out on a daily basis. Congress also took note, and in 1895, authorized a new regional mint at Denver.

Even as the gold and silver battle was being fought, plans for an international currency advanced. Europe at this time was living its own golden age, with 20 franc coins acting as its own international currency. In the era before bank wire tranfers, transactions were settled by physical shipment of gold coin across the Atlantic Ocean. Huge hoards of gold coin were held in the vaults of banks on both sides of the ocean. By the late nineteenth century, plans were in the works for an international monetary conference to deal with this and many other issues; in 1897, Congress authorized commissioners to attend the International Monetary Conference.

Throughout the 1890s and the early part of the twentieth century, many laws were passed relating to the recoinage of silver. The Mint nearly always melted down and recast gold and silver coins that had been withdrawn from circulation, and often did the same with minor coinage. Perhaps as many as a third of all the gold and silver coins ever issued went back to the melting cauldrons. Minor coinage has an equally impressive melting record— meaning that only a few such coins survive.

Coin Legislation: Commemorative Coins

At the turn of the twentieth century, commemorative coins once again moved to the forefront of coinage legislation—first with the 1899 authorization of the Lafayette commemorative half dollar and then in 1904 with the Lewis & Clark exposition dollars, the earliest in a series of gold commemorative coins that would continue throughout the Mint's second century of existence.

The entire twentieth century was an extraordinary period for American numismatics, involving profound change, significant involvement in national monetary policy, and extreme politicization. From 1791, when Congress authorized the Mint, until 1798, when certain foreign coins were given legal tender status, Congress handled only nine or so coinage-related laws. In the next hundred years, Congress enacted seventy-five coin bills,

The first commemorative dollar produced was the Lafayette Silver dollar 1899 (obverse and reverse).

as well as numerous bills relating to noncirculating medals. That number more than doubled in the twentieth century, making it the true era of commemorative coinage. The Lafayette dollar marked the beginning of a trend that continued, with some bumpy periods, throughout that century and into the next one.

From the standpoint of today's collectors, no legislation could have been as important as a congressional act of 1892, authorizing the creation of the Columbian Exposition commemorative half dollar. In the century that followed this legislation, Congress has authorized scores of other commemorative coins, most of which have had the common theme of raising revenue for a private group that is otherwise worthy of funding, but for which Congress is unwilling or unable to make direct payments from the public purse.

As common as commemorative coins may seem today, they were decidedly uncommon a century ago. The original legislation went to great pains to assure the public, and the sponsors of the various causes immortalized on the coins, that the coins would have all the properties of legal tender struck for regular circulation; in other words, they that

they could be spent. This pattern has continued until the present.

Congress passed scores of public and private laws approving issuance of national medals. Honorees ranged from the famous—such as Howard Hughes (in 1939, for his aviation achievements)—to those whose moment in history was brief—such as A. H. Rostron, the captain of the *Carpathia*, which rescued survivors of the 1912 *Titanic* shipwreck.

By 1915, Congress had authorized a half dollar, dollar, quarter eagle, and two $50 gold pieces for the Panama Pacific Exposition, the most extensive authorized commemorative coin program up to that point. These coins—designed with multiple denominations and to appeal to people at various price levels—became a model for other programs. The following year, the McKinley memorial dollar was authorized.

From passage of the Gold Standard Act of 1900 until December 1999, when Congress enacted three proposals for commemorative coin issues in the coming millennium, more than 238 separate coin initiatives (including some medals) were approved. Some of these coin laws touched the very fabric of American society.

In 1912, the American Numismatic Association (ANA) was about to enter its third decade of existence, and was rewarded with a congressional charter authorizing its activities for fifty years. President William Howard Taft signed the bill authorizing the ANA charter into law; half a century later, President John F. Kennedy renewed the charter, this time in perpetuity.

The idea of a national bank had been discarded during the Jackson administration. But President Thomas Woodrow Wilson—formerly a governor of New Jersey and a Princeton University history professor—believed differently, and in 1913, the Federal Reserve was created to solve the problem of a money supply that defied direction.

The year 1916 was a significant one numismatically, not only because of the McKinley memorial gold dollar, but because coin designs changed on the dime, quarter, and half dollar, replacing the coinage that had been circulating since 1892. No law was necessary for the new designs; a congressional act of 1890 only prohibited change, without express congressional

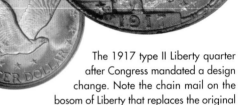

The 1917 type II Liberty quarter after Congress mandated a design change. Note the chain mail on the bosom of Liberty that replaces the original bare-breasted MacNeil design. 1917 quarters were struck with and without the mail. (obverse and reverse)

approval, if it happened more than once in twenty-five years. But once the change was made, a flap arose because of one new design: the 1916 quarter, designed by Hermon MacNeil, included a partially nude standing Liberty, with right breast exposed. Only 52,000 of the coins were produced.

The Mint, bowing to public pressure, wanted to change the coin, but claimed that the law would not allow them—the act of 1890, they declared, barred a design change more than once in twenty-five years, unless Congress directed otherwise.

1916 Liberty standing quarter (obverse and reverse). The bare breast depicted by artist Hermon MacNeil caused a scandal and congressional debate. The reverse flying eagle is fluid, dynamic, and realistic in flight. By law, the eagle must appear in all coins of 25 cents denomination and higher.

The 1909 VDB cent (obverse and reverse). Victor David Benner's initials were placed by him prominently on the reverse and removed shortly thereafter. They were restored in miniature on Lincoln's shoulder in 1918. The initials are very visible on the reverse. The obverse with the date is either plain (from the Philadelphia Mint) or bearing an "S" for San Francisco. The "D" for Denver made its first appearance in 1911.

Predictably, Congress did direct otherwise. Ohio Representative William Ashbrook was the principal sponsor of the legislation that permitted coin design modification in order to "improve" the design. (Ashbrook's other numismatic accomplishment is the establishment of the ANA's congressional charter.)

Design changes had occurred prior to 1916 without raising a public stir, such as the 1909 removal of the initials of designer Victor David Brenner from the back of the penny. (They were added to the shoulder in 1918.) There have been periodic re-engravings of the hub, sharpening of the design, and various other forms of artistic license taken by the Mint, all without congressional approval. None, in fact, probably is necessary. But it is neither the first nor the last time that the Mint's interpretation of legislation collided with political realities.

The First World War resulted in major shifts in the country's politics and economics. The numismatic consequences of the war can be seen in the passage of the Pittman Act of 1918, which caused the melting of hundreds of millions of silver dollars that had been produced before 1904, the last year that the Mint had made the coins. The silver was sent to the far east and India where it was much in demand.

Early Commemorative Coins

The year 1918 also marked the first of the many state centennial commemorative coins, as Illinois was honored with a half dollar. In 1920, commemorative coins celebrated the centennials of Maine and Alabama and the three hundredth anniversary of the landing of the Pilgrims in New England. The following year, Missouri's centennial was honored; in 1922, the centennial of the birth of general—later president—Ulysses S. Grant was marked by the creation of both a fifty cent and dollar coin, intended to benefit the restoration of the birthplace of the eighteenth president. Linking the release of a commemorative half dollar and gold dollar coin proved useful for fundraising purposes as well as a template for the future.

Lincoln commemorative half dollar 1918 for the centennial of Illinois (obverse and reverse). There will be new Lincoln commemorative cents in 2009, five in all, celebrating the life of the sixteenth president in Kentucky, Indiana, Illinois, and Washington, D.C., together with a bronze cent similar to that struck until 1982.

The Stone Mountain commemorative coin 1925, depicting Borglum's massive carving in Georgia (obverse and reverse). Borglum also designed the Mount Rushmore Memorial in South Dakota.

In 1923, the centennial of the Monroe Doctrine was honored; that same year, the New Netherlands Huguenot-Walloon three hundredth anniversary was memorialized. In 1924, the Lexington-Concord Sesquicentennial was commemorated, and Stone Mountain, Georgia, was funded with a commemorative half dollar. The following year, the Stone Mountain Association sponsors counterstamped their coins. It wasn't clear until 1993, when the James Madison Memorial Fellowship Foundation counterstruck coinage with the American Numismatic Association, that this could legally be done, and whether these coins were collectible.

A month after the Stone Mountain commemoratives, Congress agreed to memorialize the seventy-fifth jubilee of California, the hundred and fiftieth anniversary of Bennington, Vermont, and the one hundredth anniversary of Fort Vancouver. In 1926, the mother of all modern commemorative coin programs—legislation honoring the Oregon Trail—was authorized. In the years that followed, because of innovative (or inefficient, depending upon your point of view) drafting techniques, the

Oregon Trail issues continued. Oregon Trail commemorative coins were produced with many different dates and mintmarks, and probably would still be issued today if legislation enacted in 1939 had not put a halt to the practice of continuing commemorative issues.

As the nation sank into Depression, the $2.50 quarter eagle gold piece was discontinued in April 1930. But even during the Depression, dozens of commemorative coins were produced. Among these: the centennial of Texas (1933); the tricentennial of Maryland and Connecticut, centennial of Arkansas, and bicentennial of the birth of Daniel Boone (1934); the sesquicentennial of Hudson, New York and the three hundredth anniversary of Providence, Rhode Island (1935); the San Diego Exposition of 1934 and Old Spanish Trail Commemoration (1935); and the Columbia, South Carolina, sesquicentennial, Cincinnati Musical Center, and Long Island, New York, tercentenary (1936).

By the mid-1930s, President Roosevelt was heard to complain about the rate at which new

Oregon Trail commemorative half dollar (1936). Because of loopholes, the coin was also struck in 1928, 1933, 1934, 1937, 1938, and 1939. James Earle Fraser and his wife Laura Gardin Fraser prepared the designs. As a result of commemorative coin abuses, their authorization ceased in 1954 and they were not authorized again for a generation.

commemorative coins were coming out—more than one every four months. Between 1933 and 1938, a total of twenty-seven separate laws were passed by Congress that either authorized the issuance of commemorative coinage, or allowed more of a particular design to be struck. The low point, in the view of some, came in March 1936, when Congress authorized a coin commemorating the fiftieth anniversary of the Cincinnati Musical Center. The coin bears the portrait of Stephen Foster, and the slogan, "America's Troubadour." Just 15,000 coins—5,000 sets—were produced, ensuring artificial scarcity.

This explosion of commemorative issues demonstrated that the ambitions of the Mint and coin merchants far outstripped the ability of collectors and others to purchase these coins. Problems arose from the issuance of so many coins, exacerbated by overeager sponsors and unrealistically high production levels.

Legislation created and solved both problems. In 1935, Congress extended the lifetime of the Daniel Boone bicentennial commemoratives and authorized redating the coin, and also reauthorized the San Diego Exposition commemoratives in 1936. After passage of the 1939 legislation halting issuance of continuing commemoratives, there would be a few more issues, such as for Booker T. Washington and George Washington Carver. But the stage was set for the Treasury Department's termination of commemorative coin programs in 1954.

The Treasury Department had long opposed issuance of commemorative coins. Over the years, several legislative packages passed both the House and the Senate, only to be vetoed by the president. Each veto message—whether from Herbert

Glenna Goodacre

Glenna Goodacre, the sculptor whose design on the Sacagawea dollar coin is so captivating, is a native of western Texas. Although not well known to numismatists, she has been a sculptor and artist for more than a quarter century.

One of her most famous sculptures is the Vietnam Women's Memorial, adjacent to the Vietnam Veterans Memorial Wall in Washington, D.C. Her sculpture honors 11,500 American women who served in Vietnam, eight of whom were killed in combat.

Born in western Texas in 1939, Goodacre graduated from The Colorado College in Colorado Springs, Colorado. (The headquarters of the American Numismatic Association are located on that same campus today.) She received an honorary doctorate in Humane Letters from the institution in 1994.

A member of the National Sculpture Society since 1977, Goodacre won the National Academy of Design gold medal for excellence in 1978, and since 1983 has maintained a permanent studio in Santa Fe, New Mexico.

"I'll always enjoy sculpting children, different ethnic types," she says, and in one of her designs she did both: Sacagawea and young Jean Baptiste. The model was a twenty-two-year-old Shoshone woman attending college in New Mexico.

Goodacre said she sought to show Sacagawea's "spirit and her intelligence and her eagerness to lead the way." She said in an Associated Press interview that she hoped Treasury Secretary Robert Rubin would select the version with the child because "that's part of the story."

Hoover, Franklin D. Roosevelt, Harry S. Truman, or Dwight D. Eisenhower—was scripted by the Treasury Department, and emphasized that the purpose of coinage was circulation of money, not commemorative medals.

Until 1954, commemorative coins had been the

most important means of numismatic tribute. Starting in 1963, national Mint medals took that place. In the next thirty years, Congress authorized nearly 100 medals, a veritable explosion that could easily have been commemorative coinage if the intent of Congress, and the Mint itself, had not changed.

There had always been some confusion on the part of Congress as to which events were appropriate for commemorative coinage, and when a medal—even a national medal authorized by Congress—would better suffice. At least 300 separate medal laws were passed by Congress during the twentieth century—to the point where, in the 1990s, Congress momentarily lost its way and began producing coins that should have been medals, and vice versa.

For example, in 1901 Congress voted, and President Theodore Roosevelt approved, legislation authorizing bronze medals to be struck and distributed to certain officers and men who participated in the war with Spain. Nine decades later, the conflict in Korea, the Vietnam war, women in the military, World War II veterans, and prisoners of war would all be honored with commemorative coinage.

In 1904, legislation authorized that medals be struck for the centennial of the Lewis and Clark expedition. The Sacagawea dollar coin issued in 2000 bore a miniature of the Glenna Goodacre sculpture of the Indian guide to Lewis and Clark and of her young child, Jean Baptiste. Thus the same event could be memorialized in different formats (medal and coin).

In 1925, an octagonal medal was authorized to commemorate the arrival of Norse immigrants in Minnesota in 1825. The medal depicted a Viking on one side and a Viking sailing ship with the date

"A.D. 1000" on the reverse. In 1999, Congress authorized a commemorative coin marking the millennium that had passed since Leif Erikson set foot in North America. A total of 40,000 of the Norse medals were authorized, as opposed to hundreds of thousands of the commemorative coins marking the thousand years memorial.

Coined Images

Midway through his term, President Theodore Roosevelt began to correspond with a sculptor friend of his from New Hampshire, Augustus Saint-Gaudens. By the end of his term in 1909, Roosevelt left a

1912 Eagle or $10 gold piece designed by Augustus Saint-Gaudens, the noted sculptor. Weighing 0.48 troy ounces, the denomination was produced until 1933. It was revived in the 1980s for commemorative denominational use.

Reverse of the 1907 high relief by Augustus Saint-Gaudens. The eagle almost soars off the coin and comes alive. St. Gaudens had a lively correspondence with president Theodore Roosevelt over the design and kept the motto "In God We Trust" off the coin because Roosevelt thought it blasphemous.

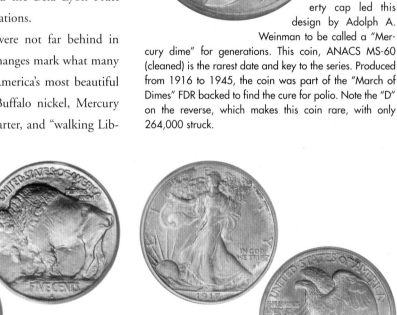

legacy of exquisite gold coinage: the Saint-Gaudens eagle and double eagle, and the Bela Lyon Pratt coinage for lower denominations.

The remaining coins were not far behind in artistic quality, and their changes mark what many still believe is the era of America's most beautiful coins: the Lincoln cent, Buffalo nickel, Mercury dime, Liberty standing quarter, and "walking Liberty" half dollar.

The winged liberty cap led this design by Adolph A. Weinman to be called a "Mercury dime" for generations. This coin, ANACS MS-60 (cleaned) is the rarest date and key to the series. Produced from 1916 to 1945, the coin was part of the "March of Dimes" FDR backed to find the cure for polio. Note the "D" on the reverse, which makes this coin rare, with only 264,000 struck.

1913-D Buffalo nickel, type I, James Earle Frasier, sculptor. The artist who did "End of the Trail" made this historic moment in miniature, still a perennial favorite among collectors. The mintmark "D" is at the 6 o'clock position on this PCGS MS-67 coin. The Mint restruck an enlarged version of the Frasier design for bullion coinage pursuant to the American Buffalo Coin Commemorative Coin Act of 2000.

This Walking Liberty half, dated 1917-S (mintmark on obverse) was also designed by Adolph A. Weinman and was part of the golden age of coinage redesign that lasted rom 1909 to about 1921. Stylish in image, flattering in perspective, the coin replaced the Barber half dollar (1916) and was produced until the Franklin half dollar started production in 1948.

The 1921 Peace dollar, designed by Anthony DeFrancisci, celebrated the end of the "war to end all wars" and has the word "Peace" emblazoned on the stone perch for the eagle on the reverse. The coin was regularly struck until 1935, and again in 1964 on orders from President Lyndon B. Johnson. The relief on this coin was too high for general circulation and was reduced in height from 1922–1935.

In 1931, anticipating the bicentennial of the birth of George Washington, Congress authorized a new quarter dollar design honoring him, replacing the standing Liberty quarter. Jean-Antoine Houdon's portrait of Washington was chosen, executed by John Flanagan. A different view of Washington, by Laura Garden Fraser, was rejected by Treasury Secretary Andrew Mellon; the design remained in the hearts of numismatists, however, and nearly seventy years later would be revived for inclusion in the commemorative coinage program honoring the two hundredth anniversary of the death of America's first president. The Jefferson nickel followed in 1938, using Felix Schlag's portrait of America's third president to start a presidential series.

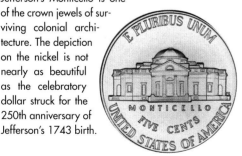

Jefferson's Monticello is one of the crown jewels of surviving colonial architecture. The depiction on the nickel is not nearly as beautiful as the celebratory dollar struck for the 250th anniversary of Jefferson's 1743 birth.

Abraham Lincoln Forever

In 2009, to mark the bicentennial of his birth, there will be at least five numismatic tributes to Abraham Lincoln, the nation's sixteenth President.

Four of the Lincoln cent designs for 2009 reflect various segments of the life of Abraham Lincoln, from his log cabin origins to his White House duties. These will be produced for circulation in copper-coated zinc. The fifth coin will be a special collector coin version made of the 1909 bronze alloy; the sixth coin for 2009 is a non-circulating silver dollar commemorative honoring Lincoln's bicentennial birthday.

Overall, there will be five 2009 cents with a "P" mintmark, five more with a "D" mintmark, at least one with an "S" mintmark sold as a proof specimen, and a copper/bronze non-circulating commemorative cent that could be produced at all four mints—including "W" for West Point.

Washington's two hundredth birthday was celebrated with this coin. John Flanagan's design replaced Laura Gardin Frasier's, which was ultimately used on the $5 commemorative for the bicentennial of his death in 1999.

Ironically, the Mint did not view the circulating quarter honoring Washington as a commemorative. But the 1931 legislation makes it clear that it is indeed commemorative, and its success as a well-known design—lasting through the 1999 implementation of the state quarter program—elevates the lowly Washington two-bit piece to the level of artistic contribution to the nation. As a workhorse of the American economy, the Washington quarter is in almost continuous circulation—a privileged position that also became true of the bicentennial commemorative quarter (1976) and the 50 state quarter program that started in 1999.

"In God We Trust"

No book on coins would be complete without discussion of Theodore Roosevelt's decision to remove the motto "In God We Trust" from the Saint-Gaudens coinage. Some have assumed it was agnosticism on the part of Roosevelt, or antipathy to organized religion. To the contrary, he was a very religious man. His piety was such that he thought it blasphemous to place the Lord's name on coinage in any context.

Congress took a very different approach: seeing the political practicalities of a godless society, it dictated that the slogan remain. The debate over these four words would climb to the U.S. Supreme Court, which would declare that the motto was "secular" and intended to impart no religiosity.

That claim was wrong, of course: The motto began during the Civil War as a direct appeal to the Almighty to assist the Union Army. A Pennsylvania minister asked Treasury Secretary Salmon Chase to place the motto on coins to show on whose side the Lord was truly on.

With the motto restored by Congress, it would be another half century before Matt Rothert, a furniture manufacturer from Camden, Arkansas (who later became president of the ANA) persuaded several members of Congress to propose legislation to place the motto on all coinage and paper money of the nation.

Money: Value and Worth

The Great Depression will probably never be forgotten by the generation that experienced it, or by their children. In 1929, just as the Depression was about to begin, the Mint produced 275 million cents. By 1933, the number was a mere twenty million. Some fifty-one million nickels were struck in 1929; by 1932 and 1933, none were struck at all.

Dimes represented real money, especially considering that in 1929 the average agricultural wage was twenty-four cents an hour; manufacturing workers earned an average of fifty-six cents hourly. That year, more than thirty-five million dimes were produced. By 1930, the number fell to eleven million. The next year was worse, with just six million from all three mints combined. In 1932 and 1933, none at all were produced.

As for quarters, the quantity minted dropped from fourteen million in 1929 to seven million in 1930, and none in 1931 or 1933. Even the George Washington bicentennial quarter in 1932 was reduced to a mere 6.2 million coins—including two rarities, the 1932-D and 1932-S quarters.

Half dollars had been produced slowly, even before the Depression. There were 1.9 million struck in 1928 and 2.9 million in 1929, but after that none were made until 1933, when just 1.7 million were produced. Silver dollars were in a hiatus, with none at all made from 1929 to 1933. Clearly, the nation was in dire economic straits.

Enter Franklin Delano Roosevelt, a distant cousin of Theodore, who was married to Teddy's niece, Eleanor. The FDR years mark a watershed in contemporary American coin collecting. He swiftly issued an executive order nationalizing gold, bringing in all but rare and unusual coins; banks were closed; and an alphabet soup of agencies began to run economic life.

By 1933, the price of gold was raised from $20.67 an ounce (a level maintained fairly steadily since 1834) to $35 an ounce. The effect of this was to make each circulating $20 gold piece worth $33.86; hence FDR's recall of hoarded coins.

The construction of Fort Knox in Kentucky to hold the gold was a front-page event in the nation's newspapers. Removal of the gold from the Federal Reserve Bank of New York and its shipment to Kentucky captured the national imagination, and would continue to do so into the 1960s, when Ian Fleming's James Bond adventure *Goldfinger* described a fictional attempt to destroy the facility.

Still later, in 1974, Dr. Peter Beter attracted congressional attention with his claim that at night, a secret transportation system was depleting the nation's gold stock—taken mostly from melted coinage—and literally sending it out the back door. An investigation ensued, together with an inspection trip of the facility—the only time Fort Knox was opened to the public. It was much ado about nothing; all of the gold was present.

The Gold Reserve Act of 1934 effectively ended gold coinage; not for another forty years would Americans even have the right to own gold, except for rare and unusual coins. This exception allowed the 1933 $20 gold piece to become a sought-after clandestine coin. The now-famous coin was produced at the Philadelphia Mint in substantial quantities before FDR's recall order, and several eventually entered circulation by means still not fully known.

As the nation responded to the needs of World War II, a congressional act of December 18, 1942 authorized the removal of copper—at the time, a critical war material—from the cent and the nickel. The act authorized substitutions that are now familiar to numismatists as the zinc cent and, as well as the silver war nickel, which added a "P" mintmark and other large mintmarks on the reverse to easily distinguish it from other nickels.

The 1955 closing of the San Francisco Mint in the name of economy directly correlated to the coin shortage of a decade later. That shortage in turn led to "clad" coinage, a devaluing of silver, and

The half cent was produced from 1793 to 1857 (obverse and reverse). At 200 coins per dollar, it was a weighty piece of change that time and inflation eventually passed by. Imagine how stores would price things today if the half cent were still produced.

a run on silver in the early 1960s that would not end until 1980, when Nelson and Bunker Hunt tried, unsuccessfully, to capture the whole silver market.

Because of rising metal prices, tin was removed as a coinage metal in 1962. In 1974, legislation was passed to allow a change over to copper plus any other metal, ultimately chosen to be zinc (99.2%) and copper (0.8%) in 1982 for the same reason. The penny is simply a placeholder, of little use in many transactions. The denomination has slid a long way since 1793, when it contained its full measure's worth of copper (and was therefore worth the metal it was printed on). In 2007 some lobbied for outright elimination of the cent as an anachronistic coin.

Meanwhile, collector coins were melted down and destroyed forever, even common-date Washington quarters worth nearly $20 in well-circulated condition. The great coin melt had begun, and the San Francisco Mint, repurposed as an assay office, was placed back on standby production alert to help stop the great coin shortage.

A belief circulated through the Treasury Department, principally fueled by Eva B. Adams, then director of the Mint, that coin collectors were largely responsible for the shortage—a belief that proved to be false. Nonetheless, the Treasury imposed punitive measures, first by obtaining legislation to freeze the date on all coins at 1964 (the ban lasted into 1965), and then deciding to eliminate mintmarks on

1857 large cent. Large cents were produced from 1793 to 1857. The act of Feb. 21, 1857 replaced it with the flying eagle cent. The size of the large cent (originally about 29 mm, later 27.5 mm) grew out of step with an increasingly mobile economy. The small cent was 19 mm in size.

1857 flying eagle cent. The large cent was replaced with a flying eagle. The 1856 coins are patterns, where this 1857 is the first year of regular issue. The model for the coins is Peter the Mint eagle; a taxidermist did his job well and the model is still found in today's Philadelphia Mint. The designer of this coin and its Indian head cent successor starting in 1859 was James B. Longacre.

JFK Half Dollar

Just sixty-nine days after President John F. Kennedy's assassination on November 22, 1963, the first Kennedy half dollar was struck. This coin is among the most collected, worldwide, by a generation of people who are not coin collectors but who admired the American leader.

On November 25, 1963, mint director Eva B. Adams telephoned Chief Engraver Gilroy Roberts at the Philadelphia Mint to advise him that a move was afoot to commemorate the slain president and to place his portrait on a U.S. coin—denomination not yet known.

A mere three days later, Roberts and Frank Gasparro did the impossible: The first trial dies were completed, and the trial strikes were hand-carried to the mint director's office. This record-breaking pace was made possible by the fact that the Mint's original models for the president's medal were available in the die shop at the Philadelphia Mint.

In a January 1964 interview, Gasparro, then an assistant engraver at the Mint with more than twenty years' service (and later chief engraver himself), reflected on the difficulty. "The reverse of the half dollar was hard to strike up at first. I had to make a deeper dish and reduce the basin on the galvano for the half dollar. I did this so that the obverse would be the first thing that would come up."

If this hadn't been done, the Kennedy portrait would have been soft, and the hair details would simply have melded into a single blob.

Roberts later wrote that Mrs. Kennedy asked for changes to the late president's hair, which Roberts said could be accomplished in the short time remaining. Back he went to Philadelphia, where he made "the part in the hair on the portrait . . . less pronounced . . . and more accents were added."

Within ten days, Roberts was en route to West Palm Beach with final trial strikes, which Jacqueline Kennedy approved on Dec. 27, 1963—all before the law authorizing the coin had been enacted.

There remained minor technical glitches in regular production, but by January 30, 1964 (a mere sixty-nine days after the assassination), production began at the Denver Mint. During the following week, Philadelphia Mint production commenced, and on February 11, 1964, formal ceremonies were conducted at the Philadelphia and Denver Mints to mark the issuance of the new coin. The legacy of the Kennedy half dollar had begun.

all coins. Mint sets and proof sets were no longer produced.

The year 1965 is a pivotal point in American coinage history. On July 23, Congress passed the Coinage Act of 1965, which removed silver from circulating dimes and quarters. It also authorized a silver-clad half dollar made of 40 percent silver, giving a nod to the silver industry interests, and recognizing the fact that the half dollar had effectively ceased to circulate. Copper/nickel-clad coinage for the dime and quarter was also authorized. The law included a strong prohibition against issuance of a silver dollar, or any dollar coin, for the next five years—a direct response to President Johnson having ordered the striking of "peace dollar" coins at the Denver Mint.

By 1967, the coin shortage was at an end, and Congress directed that mintmarks be restored. By 1968, the focus had moved from silver to gold, and the nation's 25 percent gold cover (legislation

Dwight D. Eisenhower, thirty-fourth President of the United States, is honored on this first year of issue coin. He was also honored with a commemorative silver dollar in the centennial of his birth year, 1990. The Eisenhower dollar was first struck in 1971. America's landing on the moon on July 20, 1969, as stylized by chief engraver Frank Gasparro. The eagle both complies with law requiring it on the silver dollar and recalls the name of the ship that descended to the lunar surface.

stating that 25 percent of currency in circulation had to be backed by gold) was quietly removed.

The Coinage Act of 1970 authorized the creation of the Eisenhower dollar, both as a copper/nickel circulating coin, and as a silver-clad collectible. It also authorized the federal government's General Services Administration (GSA) to sell 2.9 million rare Carson City silver dollars, which had been gathering dust in Treasury vaults for almost a century.

Contemporary Medals, Medallions, and Commemoratives

In 1971, Congress authorized the American Revolution Bicentennial Commission (ARBC) to issue bicentennial medals; at the same time, a debate raged within ARBC's Coins and Medals Advisory Panel over whether to recommend commemoratives. In October, a circulating quarter—a colonial drummer boy—was authorized, thanks to the quick legwork of John Jay Pittman, president of the American Numismatic Association, who suggested a circulating commemorative coin to Congress. A dollar and half dollar also were struck, but neither ever achieved widespread circulation. More than a generation later, the colonial drummer boy coins are still seen in pocket change; the half dollars and dollars have long since been retired. The coins all bear a unique dual date, 1776–1976.

Even as the bicentennial coin program was being conceived, an attempt was made to create a gold coin to commemorate 200 years of American freedom. It failed in the face of a veto threat by President Nixon and opposition from the

In 1975–76, America issued three circulating coins commemorating the bicentennial, each with a "1776–1976" date. Jack Ahr, Seth Huntington, and Dennis R. Williams were the amateur designers. The quarter dollar colonial drummer boy still circulates.

Federal Reserve. Private gold ownership was still illegal and the Fed feared that creation of gold coinage would create imbalance in the international economy. But as it turned out, this was one of the last anti-gold stands in a forty-year battle against the precious metal.

Medal tributes in the 1970s were important. The bicentennial medals were authorized in February 1972, and shortly thereafter the Transpo '72 Exposition was commemorated. (In earlier times, each of these events might have been seen as sufficiently important to rate a commemorative coin instead.) In 1973, the 175th anniversary of the frigate *Constitution* was commemorated on a medal, and so was baseball great Roberto Clemente, who died tragically in the Managua earthquake rescue mission. The San Francisco cable car was given national medallic commemoration, as were athlete Jim Thorpe, the International Environmental Exposition in Spokane, and the centennial of Colorado. Other medallic tributes were also passed, such as one honoring General "Chuck" Yeager's 1947 accomplishment as the first person to break the sound barrier. In 1974, Congress granted additional funds to produce silver-clad commemorative coins.

There was more good news for numismatists in 1973: Collectors were given a dramatic tool to combat counterfeiting and unauthorized reproduction of medal coins through the Hobby Protection Act. The act helped eliminate overseas counterfeits— artistically every bit as good as the originals—that were flooding the market. The law has substantially reduced the problem of unauthorized duplication of collectible coins, while simultaneously serving to designate authorized copies. The hobby act bans the reproduction of genuine numismatic items not labeled "copy."

In 1974, the composition of the cent again changed, lowering the copper content and increasing the zinc. Simultaneously, a one-time funds transfer to Eisenhower College was authorized from numismatic proceeds, which portended things to come for other denominations and other coin programs. At the time Nixon's Treasury Secretary John Connally termed the $10 price for the coin "unconscionable," and warned of the precedent set by issuing a coin and transferring a part of its profits to a private group. The remarks were more prescient than anyone at the time suspected.

In his report to Congress early in 1977, Treasury Secretary William E. Simon presented the possibility of eliminating the dollar bill and substituting a small-size dollar coin in its place;

Nineteenth-century feminist Susan B. Anthony on the new smaller-sized dollar, 1979. The law requires that an eagle appear on the reverse of all coins 25¢ in value and above. Gasparro wove that into the symbolism that the "Eagle has landed" on the moon.

in October 1978, the Susan B. Anthony dollar was approved. The coin proved to be wildly unpopular. The original design by mint chief engraver Frank Gasparro was for a superior rendering of a flowing hair Liberty, but Congress overruled it. A month later, Congress approved the American Arts Gold Medallion Act, after strong support by the ANA's president Grover C. Criswell. Once again, the Treasury Department found individuals who testified to dire economic consequences if gold were allowed in coins. Again, this proved to be a gross simplification, and when American gold eagles were authorized in the following decade (1985) they had little economic consequence.

In 1970 Congress authorized the sale of the Carson City silver dollar, disposing of nearly three million silver dollars at a hefty profit. Uncle Sam had become a coin dealer. In 1979, Congress established the most popular medal ever produced by the U. S. Mint, honoring "John Wayne America." More than 900,000 medals were sold. From the passage of the John Wayne medal until August 1985, no fewer than fifteen national medals were authorized. Recipients included Queen Beatrix of the Netherlands, Admiral Hyman G. Rickover, Fred Waring (of blender fame, and a musician), the Louisiana World Exposition, Representative Leo Ryan (murdered in the cult massacre at Jonestown, Guyana), comedian Danny Thomas, former President Harry S. Truman, NAACP head Roy Wilkins, and Vietnam veterans and those missing in action. The Truman medal could easily have been produced as a commemorative coin.

Even as these medals were being produced, however, the Mint had a change of heart relative to com-

memorative coin programs. The change might have had something to do with the upcoming 1984 Olympic games in Los Angeles, but in 1981, a law authorized production of a silver commemorative half dollar for George Washington's three hundredth anniversary. To issue a commemorative coin, a law must be passed by Congress and approved by the President. From 1954 until 1980, there was no agreement, and hence no commemorative coinage. The tercentennial of Washington's birth broke the log jam. For the first time since 1954, the Mint was producing commemoratives. The Olympic Coin Program Bill passed in 1982, allowing gold and silver commemorative coins and opening the door for an ambitious marketing scheme.

Significantly, in 1985, two pieces of legislation passed which have had a long-range impact on coin collectors: the Statute of Liberty commemorative program, which generated the largest sales of any commemorative coin program ever, and the Liberty Coin Act, which created a silver commemorative coin. The Statue of Liberty program has been used as a template in drafting virtually ever other commemorative coin bill since. One distinctive feature of the Statue of Liberty program is inclusion of a copper/nickel commemorative coin, which turned out to be the most popular commemorative coin in history, with nearly seven million pieces sold.

In 1985, a gold bullion commemorative coin was authorized, and within a short time it displaced the krugerrand and the Canadian maple leaf as the world's best-selling numismatic gold product.

The Tax Reform Act of 1981 amended the tax code to keep self-invested pension funds from purchasing rare coins. Because the effect on the coin

The Saint-Gaudens double eagle design that so fascinated Theodore Roosevelt was legislated by Congress for America's internationally acclaimed gold bullion coinage. The coin was designed as America's answer to the Krugerrand, and it succeeded. The reverse of the gold eagle bullion coin was mandated by law to be the family of eagles design by Dallas artist Mrs. Miley Busiek. The design is modern compared to the more classical obverse.

Several later pieces of commemorative coin legislation included issues honoring the 1988 Olympics, the bicentennial of Congress, and, on June 9, 1989, the United States Capitol, which was authorized to become a U.S. Mint for a single day, when a first-strike ceremony took place there.

In a nod toward coin collectors, silver coin proof sets were approved by Congress in 1990, and two generals (Schwartzkopf and Powell) were honored with national medals in 1991, following their efforts in the Gulf War. Coins commemorating the bicentennial of the White House in 1992 quickly sold out, in part because of a low mintage. Other programs included the five hundredth anniversary of Columbus's voyage, the James Madison/Bill of Rights commemorative, the Civil War battlefields program, and Olympic commemorative coin programs, especially those from the 1996 games in Atlanta, which honored not only American participation in the games, but the centennial of the Olympic games themselves.

For the U.S. Mint, perhaps the most important piece of legislation of the decade came in 1992, when the Numismatic Public

market was devastating, a 1986 tax reform act modified the blow to allow bullion coins in individual retirement accounts. However in 1986, a ban on importing Soviet gold and South African krugerrands was approved. The ban was a statement of political opposition to both the communist Soviet system and the apartheid practiced in South Africa. By the end of the decade, the Soviet Union had dissolved, and by 1993 apartheid waned. The purchasing ban was removed but even today the US market share of the American gold eagle is an overwhelming 90% of the marketplace.

The U.S. silver eagle bullion coin obverse features the design from the Walking Liberty half dollar by A. A. Weinman. The 40.6 mm size enlargement (from the 30.6 mm half dollar) turns out to be artistically pleasing. The reverse is a heraldic eagle by John Mercanti.

Enterprise Fund was created, together with a Citizens Commemorative Coin Advisory Panel.

The advisory panel's purpose was to offer advice on commemorative coins to the Secretary of the Treasury and Congress: how many should be produced of each issue, and what types of coins should be approved. The idea took off, and a coin advisory committee with a broader mandate soon succeeded the initial panel.

While the panel was under construction, Congress passed a resolution that no more than two commemorative coin issues could be authorized each year, and that the second advisory incarnation, the Citizens Commemorative Coin Advisory Committee (CCCAC), make recommendations on them.

Significant cultural events associated with coinage over the last twenty-five years of the twentieth century included reauthorization of private gold ownership; creation of commemorative bicentennial circulating coins; the 50 state quarter program; and production of the Susan B. Anthony and Sacagawea dollars.

There were many other commemorative coins authorized, including those recognizing the fiftieth anniversary of Jackie Robinson breaking baseball's color line (1997); National Law Enforcement Officers (1997); the 150th anniversary of Dolly Madison's death (1999); the bicentennial of George Washington's death (1999); the 125th anniversary of Yellowstone National Park (1999); FDR Memorial in Washington (1997); and black Revolutionary War patriots (1998).

The 50 State Quarter Program

Of the forty or so coin and medal laws passed by Congress during the past ten years, the most significant is the 50 state quarter program and its offspring: the Lewis & Clark nickels of 2004–2005, and the presidential dollar coin and first spouse program, beginning in 2007. All make significant changes on the American coinage scene.

America's 50 state quarter program—for which *Sesame Street*'s Kermit is the official "spokesfrog"—is based on an idea so special that the U.S. government has trademarked the name and concept. Over a ten-year period, the U.S. Mint has manufactured billions of circulating commemorative coins in fifty designs representing the fifty states. (The program may grow to fifty-six coins if the U.S. territories and Washington, D.C. are added.) The idea is simple: coins with certain common elements, bound together by a common theme of statehood, being produced in abundance and placed into circulation. Each of these coins bears

Sculptor Glenna Goodacre's rendering of Sacagawea and infant Jean Baptiste on the 2000 dollar coin.
Thomas D. Rogers, Sr., sculpted the soaring eagle reverse of the Sacagawea dollar. It was by far and away the most majestic of the designs that the review panel saw and complemented the Goodacre design.

the motto "In God We Trust," the Latin phrase "E Pluribus Unum" (an expression of national unity, meaning "Out of many, one"), the word "Liberty," the coin's denomination, and the inscription "United States of America." All of them have George Washington's portrait on the obverse, a modified form of the face that has appeared on the U.S. quarter since 1932. But each has a distinctive reverse design to showcase each state in the Union.

This 50 state program completes the task that the original U.S. commemorative coin program (1892–1954) began but did not see to fruition: honoring important anniversaries connected with all 50 states.

Earlier programs celebrated milestones for fifteen states and territories, but the elimination of commemoratives in 1954 prevented extending the celebration to all of the states. And, since earlier commemoratives involved silver half dollars rather than quarters, they were sold at a premium rather than circulating at face value.

Delaware, the first state, became the first 50 state quarter, in 1999. Its design pays tribute to Caesar Rodney, a Revolutionary War patriot who made a historic eighty-mile horseback ride from Dover to Philadelphia in July 1776. Rodney arrived in time to cast a decisive vote at the Continental Congress in favor of American independence.

For all its success, the 50 state quarter program is far from what was originally contemplated and proposed by the Citizens Commemorative Coin Advisory Committee ("CCCAC"). What started at the CCCAC as a modest proposal to promote "our

Delaware state quarter. The first state quarter issued shows Caesar Rodney on his historic ride in favor of independence to Philadelphia. The design fulfilled the mission of the state quarter program: to explore American history at its best.

national ideals . . . and our esteem as a nation" expanded into a coinage program that has been described as "the most tangible way to touch the lives of every American."

Few Americans are aware of how the 50 state quarter program evolved. After the Mint studied the matter, then reported back, Congress passed three separate laws before the proposal finally became a reality. Maneuvering took place behind the scenes as advocates gradually won approval for the program. These efforts ultimately persuaded the Treasury Department, the Mint, and Congress to favor a series of circulating commemorative coins.

At its very first meeting in Washington, D.C., the Citizens Commemorative Coin Advisory Committee had a less than favorable response to the commemorative quarter idea. Notes from that first meeting reflect opposition from Mint director Philip N. Diehl, based on advice from longtime

Mint staffers who still recalled fifty years of Treasury Department opposition to commemorative coinage.

Diehl's subsequent reversal of that position, in late 1994, ultimately made all the difference. In December the CCCAC recommended to Congress that a circulating commemorative coin become part of the U.S. monetary scene.

The key congressional supporter of the plan was Delaware Representative Michael Castle, chairman of the House Coinage Subcommittee. In 1995 at a Congressional hearing, after hearing testimony from Harvey G. Stack, myself, and others, he proposed fifty different coins, one for each state, over the next ten years. Silver versions also would also be produced for sale to collectors.

Delaware was the first of the United States to ratify the U.S. Constitution. On December 7, 1787—and exactly 211 years later, a coin honoring "The First State" would be struck by the U.S. Mint.

From the state quarter program came the largest coin continuity series in American history. By the time it's over, there could be 176 different, new types to collect, if you include the new presidential dollars from the Philadelphia,

Denver, San Francisco, and West Point mints, including at least one proof version. Add the "first spouse" bullion coins, and around 216 new coins were authorized in one fell swoop! Additionally there are plans for a new buffalo nickel, a $50 gold one ounce bullion coin, and new Lincoln cents with proof sets. So it's actually 231 new coins authorized in the blink of an eye.

This law takes into account some serious issues, and breaks a lot of convention. It is likely that a number of living persons will appear on the nation's coins. There's no prohibition against it, but it smacks of monarchism and reminds us of Washington's concern that placing a presidential portrait—a live or a dead one—on a coin seems somehow to go against the covenant that was first argued in Congress more than two centuries ago.

Because Washington disapproved of the use of contemporary portraits, the original Mint Act of 1792 required that American money bear a design of Liberty. That basic concept, and its simplicity, along with certain mandatory inscriptions such as the word "Liberty," the issuer (United States of America), the date—and later, "In God We Trust"—gave rise to some of the beautiful, striking,

A new presidential dollar coin series began in 2007 with George Washington. It will feature four presidents a year for at least the next 10 years. Only deceased presidents are eligible for inclusion.

and extraordinary coinage design of the late eighteenth and early nineteenth centuries.

The issue of using portraits of living ex-presidents, as well as dead ones, is similar to one that arose from the Olympic baseball coin of 1992, a silver dollar designed by John R. Deecken depicting a pitcher in a wind-up, delivering to a waiting batter. The image was of Nolan Ryan, the great baseball star, easily traceable to news photos in the identical body positions. The question arises of whether a coin or medal of a historic figure requires permission if the figure is alive (or otherwise copyrighted), or if the name, likeness, or image is trademarked.

A congressional gold medal was presented to Frank Sinatra. There's an original, but curiously, no bronze duplicates. Here's why—and by analogy, you'll quickly see the problem of a Nixon dollar coin, a Clinton dollar, or for that matter a Millard Fillmore coin. (Sinatra's case is an interesting one,

for in 1990 the name "Frank Sinatra" was trademarked by Ol' Blue Eyes himself.) The laws of at least three states—including California, where Sinatra died—afford celebrities the right of publicity in their name after their death.

That would also be true for Californians Ronald Reagan and Richard Nixon. Tennessee (where Elvis Presley lived, and where Andrew Jackson is buried, together with James Polk and Andrew Johnson), and Indiana (home of the Indy 500, and burial place of Benjamin Harrison) are other states where this right exists. The question is: who, precisely, owns and controls an image that is burned into the public memory?

The issues extend to portraiture as well. The portraits of Elvis Presley and Marilyn Monroe on postage stamps come to mind, as does President Kennedy's portrait on national coinage and public (and private) medals—as well as those of the other American presidents.

In the 1990s and early twenty-first century, Congress backed off on issuing many noncirculating commemorative coins, such as a series

This commemorative was authorized to celebrate Thomas Jefferson's 250th birthday. The date on the coin (1993) is not the year it was struck (1994). Monticello Reverse from the Jefferson 250th anniversary commemorative. The original drawings showed the steps at a slightly different perspective.

One new commemorative of note is the 2006 Franklin tricentennial commemorative coin. It commemorates Franklin as a youth and a wise older man. Franklin was intimately involved in numismatic matters prior to the establishment of the U.S. Mint and printed some continental currency.

honoring various religious leaders, who instead were presented with congressional gold medals (Lubuvitcher Grand Rebbe Menachim Mendel Schneerson in 1994; the Rev. Billy Graham and his wife Ruth in 1996; Pope John Paul II in 2000, among others). Bronze copies are called national medals and may be purchased from the U.S. Mint.

Commemorative coins did continue, including a set in 1996 on the occasion of the sesquicentennial of the founding of the Smithsonian Institution. A surprise groundswell of support in Congress came in 2005 for the 2007 silver dollar commemorating the fiftieth anniversary of school desegregation in Little Rock, Arkansas.

For the most part, commemoratives with obscure or artificial themes sell less well than those with true historic content. The White House bicentennial (1992), Jefferson's 250th anniversary (1993), and the 225th anniversary of the Marine

Corps (2005) were sell-outs at 500,000 coins, where the bisesquicentennial of the birth of Chief Justice John Marshall sold 40 percent of that amount. The same is true for two coins honoring the three hundredth anniversary of the birth of Benjamin Franklin.

From gold and silver to base metal and back to precious metals again, a 2,800-year history of coinage continues, of which coinage of the United States of America is a small but fascinating part. To honor people, to express ideas and egalitarian concepts, and to record history: the same is true today as at the beginning of numismatic history.

CHAPTER THREE

THE COIN,
UP CLOSE AND PERSONAL

Every traditional coin has three sides, or surfaces: an **obverse**, or face; a **reverse**, or back; and an **edge**, which can be plain, reeded, decorative or lettered. This is as true for coins struck in Lydia more than 2,500 years ago as for those of 2007, when edge-lettering was revived on the new presidential dollar coin.

Within those surfaces are defined parts. There is usually, but not always, a date. On most (but not all) American coins, the date appears on the obverse. That's because the appearance of American coinage is statutorily defined: Back in 1792, Congress directed that the date appear on the obverse. It also directed that a portrait "emblematic of Liberty" appear on the face of the coin, and that the word "Liberty" also be imprinted on the front of each piece of American money.

Still later, Congress added another requirement to the face of most coins: the national motto, "In God We Trust."

For the reverse, or flip side, of most American coins, Congress requires a statement of national origin ("United States of America"); the Latin motto "E pluribus unum," meaning "out of many, one" because the thirteen colonies became one United States; and the denomination, almost always spelled out—"One Cent," "One Dol.," "Five D.," "3 Dollars" and so forth—

OPPOSITE: The Panama-Pacific Exposition commemorative, 1915.

without a dollar sign appearing. For denominations over a dime, an eagle must be depicted.

Rules can be changed by the rulemaker—Congress—such as when the 50 state quarter program was initiated. And for good reason: the mottoes and design elements required by law, and placed by legislators and not artists, make for too much clutter on a small circular planchet.

Congress regulates those elements, too. Though collectors traditionally refer to diameter dimensions of coins in millimeters, we are not a metric nation as Congress legislates the size of coins. Here's a convenient chart showing the size of current American circulating coinage:

Denomination	Size
cents	21.2 mm
10 cents	17.9 mm
25 cents	24.3 mm
50 cents	30.6 mm
1 dollar	26.5 mm

If coins are history you can hold in your hand, it is a large history on a small planchet. Congress recognized that the 50 state quarter program would be difficult to accomplish if the eagle was on the reverse—the location it had mandated for the state-representative design—so it eliminated that requirement. Other statutory inscriptions were moved around. Washington's portrait in restyled form was retained, but the date was moved to the reverse. "United States of America" was moved to the obverse, as was the denomination. "E pluribus unum" was kept on the reverse, but reduced in size.

2001 North Carolina state quarter. America's state quarter program is one of the most successful continuity programs ever devised. There are a total of fifty different designs struck, one every ten weeks, or a total of five coins a year for ten years. The program began in 1999 and concludes in 2008.

But even with the improved planchet and heightened flan size, artists complained that designs were hard to portray. So for the next large series—the presidential dollar series—the date, mintmark, "In God We Trust" motto, and "E pluribus unum" are moved to the third side, the edge. It allows the portrait to be larger and on the reverse, a larger portrait of the Statue of Liberty, and an unusual denomination, "$1."

The trade dollar never was intended to circulate domestically but still had various mottoes and legends typical of all American coins.

New presidential dollars are the first American coins to have the denomination with a dollar sign ($). Earlier coins used the phrase One Dol. or Dollar.

Because coins stay with us for so long—we can easily look back to the coinage of Caesar—political leaders and governments have spent an inordinate amount of time detailing requirements of what must appear on a nation's coinage.

Foreign countries' coinage laws are equally intricate. The Swiss coinage law of 1952, for example, details that gold coins and the silver 5 franc coin shall have "inscribed" rims, where other silver coins will have "milled" rims. Copper-nickel and bronze coins have unmilled rims. Diameters are specified in millimeters ranging from 16 mm for 1 centimes to 31 mm for the 5 franc coin.

By proclamation dated February 12, 1817, King George III

This silver crown of King George III, dated 1818, was struck according to the specifications of a Royal proclamation. King George was on the throne when America declared its independence forty-two years earlier.

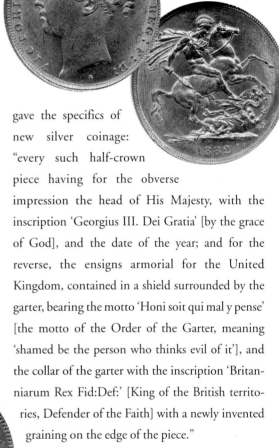

Jubilee sovereign of Queen Victoria, 1887, with reverse showing St. George slaying the dragon. Victoria's long reign resulted in her coinage portraiture being different than most monarchs. You literally can watch her age as her portrait changes.

gave the specifics of new silver coinage: "every such half-crown piece having for the obverse impression the head of His Majesty, with the inscription 'Georgius III. Dei Gratia' [by the grace of God], and the date of the year; and for the reverse, the ensigns armorial for the United Kingdom, contained in a shield surrounded by the garter, bearing the motto 'Honi soit qui mal y pense' [the motto of the Order of the Garter, meaning 'shamed be the person who thinks evil of it'], and the collar of the garter with the inscription 'Britanniarum Rex Fid:Def:' [King of the British territories, Defender of the Faith] with a newly invented graining on the edge of the piece."

In 1871, Queen Victoria issued a proclamation on January 14 changing the reverse of the sovereign, a gold coin containing 0.2354 troy ounces of gold: "the image of St. George armed, sitting on horseback, attacking the Dragon with a sword, his spear having been broken in the encounter; and the date of the year."

This silver quarter of 1796 has light adjustment marks on the reverse. The planchet was weighed and then a rasp used to reduce the weight to conform to the law before striking the final design.

There are a number of other design elements or parts of a coin that are fairly well standardized. **Exergue** is the space on a coin or medal, usually below the central design and often giving the date of issue. **Adjustment marks** commonly found on older gold and silver coins are evidence of filing down an overweight planchet to bring a coin down to legal weight. **Weight** of a coin, usually given in grains or grams, is its gross weight. **Troy weight** gives the weight of gold or silver in a coin at 12 ounces to the pound, calculated by multiplying gross weight by fineness. **Fineness** is the ratio in a precious metal coin that the precious metal bears to the whole. Most U.S. coins are .900 fine silver and gold; British sovereigns are .9167 fine.

Portrait or **effigy** usually appears on the obverse of a coin and can be singular or **jugate**, meaning two portraits conjoined—such as the Eisenhower 1990 commemorative which shows him both as a general and as President.

Field is that portion on obverse and reverse which is not covered with the principal design. **Mintmark** is a letter or symbol on U.S. coins showing where a coin is minted, for example "P" for Philadelphia, "D" for Denver," and so forth. **Hallmark** is a symbol of fineness. **Privy mark** is an indication of who was the mintmaster in charge when coins were produced. **Device** is a design on a coin other than portraiture, such as mintmark, wildlife, scenery, etc. A **secondary device** on a coin refers to a design other than the primary design. **Statutory inscriptions** are mottoes or verbiage that appear on a coin because the law so requires. **Flan**, or **planchet**, is the metal disc imprinted with the coin design. **Incused design** is a design

Thirty-fourth President and General of the Armies Dwight D. Eisenhower. Eisenhower in an unusual jugate view by John Mercanti. Eisenhower was also on a circulating dollar coin from 1971–1978.

1864 two cent piece with "In God We Trust" motto. The motto was added during the Civil War to show that the deity was on the side of the North.

recessed into the coin's surface. **Metal composition** is how a struck coin appears: as clad-coinage (the U.S. quarter dollar), as one metal plated with another (the cent), as solid gold (a 24 karat bullion coin), or otherwise. **Initials** are usually those of the engraver or sculptor who designed the coin and reproduced it in die form.

Minting

The primary purpose of all coinage is to circulate as a medium of exchange, a legal tender. This means that you can use the coin at the candy store, at a bank, to pay your local taxes, or for any debt, public or private. For the past 150 years, however, there has been a secondary purpose for coinage: to satisfy collectors. This involves the minting and manufacture of proof coinage.

Both modern proof issues and circulation strikes use essentially the same dies and machinery to produce the result—a coin—and the resulting coins appear at first blush to be identical. But on closer examination, the proof and uncirculated coin are as much alike as a lithograph is to an original piece of art.

Minting of circulation strikes at a modern mint is essentially the same whether it is at s'Rijks Munt in Utrecht, the Netherlands, the United States Mint at Philadelphia, the Casa de Moneda of Mexico, La Zecca in Rome, the British Royal Mint in Scotland, or any private mint that does commercial or other production of legal tender or commemorative coins. These steps, in turn, may be more modern and take advantage of twenty-first century technology, but essentially the work is the same as it was more than 2,000 years ago in ancient Greece.

Charles Barber, Chief Engraver of the U.S. Mint

Charles Barber's family emigrated to the United States from England in 1852, when Charles was twelve. His father, William Barber, became chief engraver of the U.S. Mint, serving from 1869 to 1879. At the age of 29, Charles followed his father, serving as assistant engraver at the Philadelphia Mint.

When the senior Barber died in 1879, President Hayes nominated Charles Barber to become the new chief engraver; he was confirmed by the Senate on January 20, 1880.

Barber's lifetime of achievement is memorialized in numismatic lore by more than the coinage that bears his name: the Barber dime, Barber quarter and Barber half dollar, all struck starting in 1892. There is the less-well known Barber nickel, known in numismatic circles as the Liberty head nickel, struck from 1883 to 1912, together with five examples dated 1913.

Barber was the artist for at least seven commemorative coins and also produced medals awarded to twenty-eight different years of Assay Commission members. He designed at least twenty-nine different medals produced by the Mint on topics ranging from presidential and mint director portraits, to Indian peace and lifesaving medals.

In addition to his artistic achievements, Charles Barber was a chronicler of his life and times, an inveterate saver of correspondence he both received and sent. He also collected examples of the coins that he created, and the patterns that he designed—together with examples of the work of others.

In November, 1991, the Smithsonian Institution received an extraordinary gift from Harvey, Norman, and Lawrence Stack: the personal papers of Charles Barber, covering his term as sixth chief engraver of the United States Mint at Philadelphia.

Organized by category, Barber's papers include handwritten correspondence, typescripts, and many design sketches for various coins. They cover coinage of the United States and many foreign countries, medallic works by the artist, and his extraordinary collection of numismatic pattern pieces, one of the finest ever assembled.

Elements

The essential elements of the process of minting a coin are a minting facility, and a source for raw materials. Some mints do their own processing; others, like the United States Mint, produce some planchets—such as for clad coinage (dime, quarter, half dollar)—but buy ready-to-strike golden dollar blanks (from Olin Brass, among others) or copper-plated zinc cents, also bought on competitively bid contracts.

There are at least seven distinct stages to the manufacture of every circulating coin. Each coin is (1) blanked, producing a planchet without a rim, empty of design; (2) annealed or heated; (3) upset, raising the rim on the coin; (4) struck; (5) inspected; and finally, (6) counted and bagged, shipped or stored.

Blanking

The U.S. Mint buys copper/nickel clad strips of metal, approximately thirteen inches wide and 1,500 feet long, to manufacture the dime, quarter, half-dollar, and dollar. The same specifications apply to the nickel (made of a 75 percent copper/25 percent nickel alloy) and the golden dollar (a copper/zinc/manganese/nickel alloy). The strips, which come tightly rolled in a coil and

Webbing from the blanking process. The coins are punched out as blanks from a larger rolled metal sheet; the blanks are then fed to the coining press to complete production.

weigh about three tons each, are delivered to the Mint's production area looking like an oversized donut the size of a young adult. Each coil is lifted onto a spindle that feeds directly into a blanking press, which punches out round, plain-surfaced disks, called cut blanks, from the strip.

The highest-tonnage blanking press is used to punch out a nickel; a dime-sized blank requires the least amount of pressure. Each blank is cut slightly larger than the final coin size in order to allow for the formation of the rim, but the weight of the blank is the same as the final authorized coin weight.

Leftover strip, called webbing, is shredded and recycled; some limited quantities have reached the secondary market and are admired, and acquired, by collectors.

To manufacture one cent coins—which the Mint does to the extent of 14 billion pieces a year, or 70 percent of its production—the Mint buys ready-made planchets after supplying fabricators with copper and zinc.

Annealing

The blanks are then heated in an annealing furnace to soften them. The temperature is at least 1,400 degrees Fahrenheit for clad coinage, less for the zinc cent whose melting point is 787 degrees Fahrenheit. The temperature discolors the planchet, making it appear dull and grey; to give the future coin the shiny surface that the public expects, it is given a soapy chemical bath. From the annealing furnace, the heated blanks drop into a quench tank to reduce the temperature. Then the blanks travel through a huge cylindrical tube called the whirlaway, which tilts at a severe 45-degree angle toward the washing and drying station. As the blanks travel the whirl-away toward the washer, excess liquid is drained.

Leaving the whirlaway, blanks are placed in a commercial washing machine. There are a series of cycles that soak and shake the blanks in various chemicals, removing oxides, tarnish, discoloration, or contamination that may remain after the annealing.

Frank Gasparro

Frank Gasparro served as chief engraver of the United States Mint for sixteen years—1965 to 1981—a modest tenure for the modest man who was the tenth person to hold the position since it was established with the founding of the Mint in 1792.

One of his greatest designs was the flowing haired Liberty small-sized dollar, created as a pattern in 1976–1977 in anticipation of the reduction in size of the dollar coin (which ultimately came about in 1979).

Gasparro's coinage work include the Lincoln Memorial reverse of the cent; the reverse of the Kennedy half dollar; the Susan B. Anthony dollar (obverse and reverse); and the Dwight D. Eisenhower dollar coin, as well as contemporary commemorative coinage.

Upsetting

The next step in the process is to give the coin a rim or edge, its third side. The blanks go through an upsetting mill, which raises a rim around their edges, turning the blanks into planchets. For most coins, reeding the edge is done during the striking process; some mints do it during the upsetting process. For U.S. coins, the upsetting simply raises the rim smoothly, so that the planchet is coin-sized and fits into the coining press collar. At the Royal Canadian Mint, edge-lettering is done manually, coin for coin, on dollar-sized commemoratives.

Striking

Planchets are brought by conveyor belt to the coining press for striking. The edge lettering on the presidential coins is placed on the coins during striking, and should all be in the same position on each coin. The collar die incusing the edge lettering is a three-part segmented collar that closes during striking and retracts afterward. If a reeded edge is required, it is applied to the planchet during coining by a collar inside the coining press. Production strikes run at a rate of 600 to 750 coins per minute, depending on which coin is being produced. Multiple dies can be done on a single coining press—where the image is struck on the obverse and reverse at the same time—for smaller-sized coins like the U.S. dime or cent; the U.S. half dollar is struck one-up.

Inspection

Once a coin is struck, there is an inspection process—not for every coin, but a spot check. There is the visual check, eye-to-coin, and a magnifying glass to spot-check each batch of new coins.

Counting and Bagging

An automatic counting machine counts the coins and drops them into bags. The bags are sealed, loaded on pallets, and taken by forklifts to be stored. New coins are shipped by truck to Federal Reserve Banks for counting. From there, the coins go to local banks and into circulation.

Proof coins

Proof coins are intended for collectors and go through all of the above steps plus a few extras: the planchets are polished to a mirror finish, and the coins are struck on hydraulic presses twice, to bring up the coin design. The coins are handled individually, with all mint staff wearing gloves to prevent contact with hand oils. It is a common error among inexperienced collectors to term "proof" a grade or condition, when "proof" refers to a method of manufacture. Proof coins, like uncirculated coins, have different gradations. Generally, on the 1 to 70 grading scale that is in widespread use (with 70 being the best), a proof coin is numerically described as proof-60 (or pf-60) to proof-70, unless it is mishandled, in which case it could be a

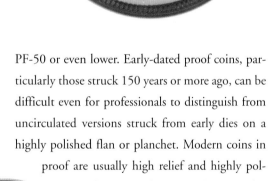

This 1875 $3 gold piece in NGC Proof-64 condition is an example of proof production. Three dollar gold pieces were produced from 1854 to 1889, but never in large quantities. The 1875 was produced as a proof only coin (as was 1876).

PF-50 or even lower. Early-dated proof coins, particularly those struck 150 years or more ago, can be difficult even for professionals to distinguish from uncirculated versions struck from early dies on a highly polished flan or planchet. Modern coins in proof are usually high relief and highly polished, compared to a circulation strike. The mirror-like finish is usually the give-away.

Proof coin. All proof coins are specially struck for collectors and are not intended for general circulation. They are struck at least twice mirrorlike planchets.

CHAPTER FOUR

WHAT TO COLLECT

I f you're like some new collectors, you might feel a desire to strike it rich from coins found in your pocket change. That's always been one attraction of numismatics. The beautiful thing about collecting coins is that there is no correct or incorrect way to do it; there are as many ways to collect coins as there are coins to collect. The key is to set a goal as to what you want to collect, and why.

Some people enjoy completing a set, and use an old-fashioned album they fill in, coin by coin, until it is complete. (Commercial albums are available, enabling the collector to organize, for example, Lincoln cents from 1909 to 1940, 1941 to 1958, and the Lincoln Memorial series from 1959 to date.)

Type collecting can be limited to circulating coinage of the twentieth century, or circulating minor coinage (cents and nickels), or subsidiary coinage (dimes, quarters, and half dollars), or dollar coins of the twentieth century or an earlier period. (For collectors who want to experience the designs of all of America's coinage by type, there are holders and albums designed to accommodate that, too.) As an example, let's look at fifteen different ways you can collect and acquire state quarters:

OPPOSITE: 2007 United Kingdom £1 Silver Proof and four-coin gold proof bridge collection, struck by the British Royal Mint.

The state quarter program designs do not have a uniform theme except as to the positioning of the date, the state, and various mottos and legends. Some designs use outlines of state maps, others don't. The governor of each state made the recommendation.

- By date and mintmark (i.e., 1999 P, D, S)
- By all five coin issues (a 150-coin complete set)
- By date only (a 50-coin complete set)
- By circulated coin issues (i.e., Philadelphia and Denver mint, a 100-coin complete set)
- By proof coin regular issue only (i.e., "S" mint only set containing 50 coins)
- A silver-coin-only set (proof only, "S" mint, a 50-coin set)

- Alphabetically by state (Alabama, Alaska, Arizona, Arkansas, etc.)
- By design, such as those showing state maps: Pennsylvania, Georgia, South Carolina, Ohio, Indiana, Louisiana, Illinois, Michigan, Texas, Minnesota, etc.
- By those depicting natural phenomena, such as the Connecticut charter oak tree, New Hampshire's late Old Man of the Mountain, Vermont maple trees, etc.
- By those depicting animals, such as Delaware's horse bearing Caesar Rodney, South Carolina's Carolina wren, Louisiana's pelican, Wisconsin's cow, the California eagle, Kansas's bison, Nevada's wild mustangs, North Dakota's bison, etc.
- By historical figure, such as Delaware's Caesar Rodney, New Jersey's Washington crossing the Delaware, the Massachusetts Minute Man, Ohio's Neil Armstrong, Illinois's Lincoln, Alabama's Helen Keller, California's John Muir, etc.
- By error. There are an amazing number of double and triple struck state quarter coins and a collection of them, although expensive to acquire, is fascinating to look at side by side.

State quarter reverse from Pennsylvania, Ohio, Louisiana, and Texas. The distinctive nature of the designs is evident in this selection that includes the keystone state (1787, Pennsylvania) and the Lone Star State (1845, Texas).

State quarter errors include these multiply-struck, off-center Georgia coins, a Pennsylvania coin struck on the wrong planchet, an off-center New Hampshire coin, a weakly struck Tennessee coin and a Kansas coin missing cladding.

- With other coins struck in honor of one or more of the 50 states. The U.S. Mint, at the behest of Congress, struck commemorative coins honoring the statehood of a number of states, ending with Iowa in 1946. These include: Alabama, Arkansas, California, Connecticut, Delaware, Illinois, Iowa, Maine, Maryland, Missouri, Oregon, Rhode Island, Texas, Vermont, and Virginia. Each state issue required a separate act of Congress and approval of the President; the coins are legal tender but are not intended for circulation.
- Roll sets
- By designer

Two different approaches to honoring a state are evident in the Arkansas 1936 commemorative coin and the Arkansas state quarter.

1794 Silver dollars. Even a VF-25 coin as shown here is now expensive. This coin sold in a Heritage auction in January, 2007 for $126,500.

1878 Morgan dollar (eight tailfeather variety) NGC Ms-66. With silver in abundance, millions of silver dollars were made with the George Morgan design between 1878 and 1921.

Alternatively, you may want to collect dollar coins. The following dollar coins offer an interesting look at American history:

- Flowing haired Liberty dollars, 1794–1795. The 1795 is the affordable one, in circulated condition; the uncirculated ones are very expensive. The design of Liberty is a young independent woman—like the nation she represents.
- Draped bust Liberty (1795–1804), and small eagle reverse 1795–1798, depicting a more mature Liberty but a puny eagle defending the nation.
- Heraldic eagle reverse (1798–1804), with the eagle from the Great Seal's beak pointed toward the arrows of war and away from the olive branches of peace. Again, most affordable in circulated condition.
- Liberty seated dollars (1840–1865), with a Liberty looking westward and the eagle's talons holding arrows and olive branches.
- Liberty seated with motto "In God We Trust" on reverse.
- Trade dollar (1873–1885). Originally not legal tender (it obtained that status in 1965, almost a century later), it shows a mature Liberty about

1866 "with motto" dollar, PCGS proof-64 cameo. Silver dollars did not circulate widely, nor was there a demand for them, prior to 1870. The "Crime of '73" was mostly in response to the discovery of the Comstock Lode, huge silver deposits.

1921 Peace dollar. This coin design by Anthony DeFrancisci replaced the Morgan dollar design in 1921. The "flapperish" portrait of Liberty matched the mood of the nation, replacing the more matronly and Victorian dollar design of the last century. The Morgan design was used in the twentieth century from 1900–1904 and again in 1921.

to be a world traveler. The eagle's beak is pointed toward the olive branches.

- Morgan silver dollar (1878–1921) shows a Victorian lady, plump and mature, and a peaceful if vigilant eagle.
- Peace dollar (1921–1935). Liberty is depicted as a flapper; the word "Peace" appears on the coin beneath the eagle on the reverse.
- Eisenhower dollar (1971–1978), with the thirty-fourth President of the United States in a Roman style portrait and a reverse celebrating the 1969 Lunar landing.
- Bicentennial dollar, 1976. With the Liberty Bell superimposed on the moon, no eagle.
- Susan B. Anthony dollar (1979–1999).
- Sacagawea dollar (2000 to date). Glenna Goodacre's award-winning design.
- Presidential dollars (2007–2018). A portrait gallery.

There are even ten gold coins that you can buy for under one hundred dollars each that ought to be desired by every collector, as they are genuinely scarce and likely to increase in value in the coming years.

Coin collecting is fun, profitable, and lucrative. Naturally, each of these sample lists is no guarantee of future increases in value, but each certainly has

This 1970-S NGC Proof-66 sold for $24 on February 13, 2007. In 1970, no halves were made for circulation; only collector-coin versions were minted.

Statue of Liberty commemorative gold coin. This 1986-W, contains the mintmark of West Point. The Statue of Liberty program was one of the most successful commemorative marketing efforts in modern times.

the potential to reach for the stars and jump auspiciously in the not-too-distant future.

Government Issue Examples

America's most wanted modern Mint issues struck since 1970, priced under $400 at issue:

Date & Mintmark	Denomination	Mintage & statistics
1970-D	Half dollar	2,150,000 issued only in mint sets
1970-S	Half dollar	2,632,810
1984-P, D, or S	$10 Olympic coin	P 33,309; D 34,533; S 48,551
1992-S	Silver 10¢, 25¢, and 50¢ coin	1.3 million
1986-W	$5 Statue of Liberty coin	Uncirculated mintage 95,248
1988-W	$5 Olympic coin	Uncirculated mintage 62,913
1989	Gold $25 coin	Half ounce mintage 44,829

Elizabeth Jones, chief engraver of the U.S. Mint, sculpted this ethereal vision of Nike, a 1988-W Olympic commemorative coin. The reverse is Marcel Bovine's stylized Olympic flame.

Belgian Cartoon Coin

In 2004, Belgium minted a silver 10 euro coin to celebrate the seventy-fifth birthday of Tintin, its cartoon hero. The first coin was struck in the presence of Fanny Rodwell, the widow of the pint-size reporter's creator Hergé, ahead of the actual anniversary on January 10, 2004.

One of Belgium's most recognized figures, Tintin, with his faithful dog Snowy, was born in January 1929 in a children's supplement to the *Vingtieme Siecle* ("twentieth century") newspaper.

Hergé's satire on the Soviet state was very much a part of its time. Soviet propaganda designed to persuade the world outside Russia that their economy was booming was a particular target for Hergé, as were the activities of the OGPU, the secret police.

Tintin's first adventure was followed by twenty-three full-length books, which have been translated into fifty languages with some 200 million copies sold worldwide. The cartoon books and related merchandising—much of which is sold to tourists visiting Belgium—have become the center of a multi-million euro industry.

Proof Sets: Just for Collectors

One of the best potentialities for any collector or investor has to be contemporary proof sets, bought in the secondary market rather than from the Mint itself and usually at a lower price than that of issue.

This is also true of modern commemorative coins, purchased on the secondary market about a year after issue, when the marketing efforts of the Mint have collapsed and the price is about half of what it was when it was originally sold to collectors.

Mintage of proof sets averages around three million cents a year—relatively high from a historic standpoint, but low relative to the number of potential collectors. Most importantly, each set contains a number of coins produced only at that Mint with that mintmark.

For a collector to have a complete set of Lincoln cents, Jefferson nickels, Roosevelt dimes, Washington quarters, or Kennedy half dollars, she *must* have a proof set (or a broken version of it). Some dates and mintmarks (like the 1970-S half dollar) were never struck for circulation and are available only in proof sets, which must be broken to accommodate collector's storage and display issues.

A 1984-S nickel or dime may not sound especially rare, with 3.065 million minted (2.7 million proof pieces minted for the proof set and 300,000 for the prestige set). By contrast, the 1984-D nickel had 517 million pieces produced. The last time that around three million nickels were produced was in 1950, at the Denver Mint. Before that, there was the 1931-S (1.2 million). But each is a "key" coin. This affords a significant opportunity to both

Specimen or proof sets are made by mints the world over. This set for King George VI of England was produced during his first full year on the throne (Edward VIII having abdicated as King in 1936). Note how the Royal Mint uses color, size and shape of different coin denominations to easily facilitate recognition.

the collector and the investor, and, given the modest prices for many of the issues, shows that the sky is potentially the limit.

The 1970 Denver and San Francisco half dollars are another story. Being the first of the modern half dollars that were produced only for collectors, they created a modern rarity in the process. Nearly a quarter century later, they are an underappreciated rarity with mintages of 2.1 and 2.6 million, respectively. The New Orleans and Philadelphia mints made more half dollars in 1854, in 1826, and many other years in between.

Just 2.6 million proof coins were minted compared to 2.1 million uncirculated 1970 halves, none of which were intended for circulation, and all of which were produced for mint sets manufactured by the United States Mint that year.

Originally sold to collectors, and only as part of the official Mint or Proof sets, these coins have long since been broken out because of their low mintages, but nonetheless are available in relatively limited quantities.

It is unlikely, for example, that someone would put together as many as 100,000 coins, or even as many as 20,000. Thus, it is a coin that could be mass-marketed, but also has substantial appeal to collectors.

Commemorative Coins

Modern commemorative coin issues are something every serious collector ought to consider. Just because they aren't bought from the Mint—they are available, frequently, on the aftermarket for less than the issue price—doesn't mean that they can't be topical, fun, and sometimes eventually lucrative.

In fact, the uncirculated versions—rather than the proofs—almost always cost less and seem to have much lower mintages, meaning that they can have investment potential to the person willing to buy now and hold onto the coin for the foreseeable future. Their mintage is about one third of the typical proof piece. So while a 1995 Civil War dollar came close to selling out with about 500,000 pieces sold, 437,000 were proofs and only 45,000 were uncirculated. The 2006 Benjamin Franklin tricentennial has 142,000 proofs compared to 58,000 uncirculateds.

Greg Louganis

Greg Louganis, the 1984 and 1988 Olympic diving champion, collected over forty national diving titles in the short span of a dozen years. His awards include six Pan American gold medals, five world championships, and multiple Olympic gold medals.

Coins struck honoring Louganis include a $100 gold coin depicting him standing on the ten-meter platform, ready to undertake one of his amazing performances, and a series of three $25 silver coins showing the graceful dives of the American champion, one of which is so real in appearance that he seems to be diving off the sheen of the proof surface.

Each of the coins is struck as a proof, and also in uncirculated, by Sunshine Mining in Coeur d'Alene, Idaho. All are legal tender in the Republic of the Marshall Islands.

Each of the coins commemorating Louganis has been skillfully engraved by Walter Ott, formerly master engraver at the Royal Canadian Mint. The obverse features Louganis in a diving position; the reverse depicts the Great Seal of the Republic of the Marshall Islands.

Contemporary commemorative coins—especially gold issues—are extraordinary buys, especially when placed in historical perspective. The 1926 sesquicentennial commemorative ($2.50) coin had a mintage of 46,019 pieces—and a half century or more later, there are any number of commemoratives with lower mintages. The 1984-P (33,000) and 1984-D (35,000) Olympic $10 commemorative is one design in point.

But even comparing regular issues with commemoratives (a dangerous exercise), the Statue of Liberty 1986 coin with Elizabeth Jones's arresting portrait of the Statue's face has but 95,248 pieces produced in uncirculated.

Of all the half eagle coins produced in prior years, only the 1911-D (mintage of 72,500), the 1909-O (34,200) and the 1980-S (82,000), all key coins, have lower mintages than the 1986 noted above.

The 1989-D uncirculated Congress silver dollar commemorative (mintage 135,203) has a lower mintage than any previous silver dollar produced during the twentieth century (including Morgan, Peace, Ike, and Anthony series), and when considering the entire Morgan series dating back to 1878, only three coins have a lower mintage: the 1895 (a proof only issue, and scarce), 1893-S, and 1894—each of which is rare and pricey.

Perhaps the best finds among modern issues are the Mint's own errors—the S-less proof coins manufactured, irregularly, since 1968. These include the 1968 no-S dime, 1970 no-S dime, 1971 no-S nickel, 1975 no-S nickel, 1983 no-S dime, and 1990 no-S cent.

Proof coin production resumed in 1968 after a three year hiatus, moving from the Philadelphia Mint to San Francisco. In start up, a small error: the 1968 no-S proof dime, a rare San Francisco Mint error.

A 20 lire coin of Italy's King Umberto I from 1882, in uncirculated condition, sells for barely more than its gold weight at about $150, while a 5 franc coin of Napoleon III can be obtained in VF/VI in the range of about $100.

Examples of gold coins available in the $150 price range (with gold at $650 an ounce): Australia old sovereign (1918); Belgium 20 francs; Chile 100 pesos 1898 (Friedberg *Gold Coins of the World* catalogue number 52); Czechoslovakia 1 ducat 1923; France 5 francs 1863A (Friedberg number 558); Great Britain half sovereign, 1887; Hungary 20 korona 1897 (Friedberg 92); Italy 20 lira 1882-R (Friedberg 21); Newfoundland $2, 1888; and Switzerland 20 francs 1911B (Friedberg 499).

These are real coins, some of which were used, hence their circulation factor. Others were used

Each was available from the Mint—accidentally—at costs ranging from $5 to $11, and each has a considerable worth. Generally, only a few thousand pieces were produced before the error was discovered and rectified.

Affordable Gold Coinage

Gold is the stuff of legend, lore, glory, and war. But gold coinage is not necessarily expensive. Even with gold at $650 an ounce, there are still at least 91 different coins from nations around the world, from Albania to Yugoslavia, that can be acquired for under $350. There are also at least ten countries which have gold coins available for $200 or less, making it a very affordable collectible.

British sovereigns—each containing .2354 ounces of gold—or half sovereigns include Queen Elizabeth II, King George VI, George VI, Edward VII, and Queen Victoria in the twentieth century. Many of these coins are in the $170 and up range.

There are many highly collectible gold coins, such as this 1887 half sovereign, that are available at moderate cost, principally because the gold coins that originally circulated were designed not to be too heavy to use.

U.S. Paper Money

Twelve of the thirteen original colonies produced their own paper currency, but the continental currency failed ("not worth a continental" was the phrase of the day). By the time the federal Constitution was adopted in 1789, there was a prohibition against anything other than gold or silver being legal tender—a direct response to hyperinflation during the Revolutionary War.

America's experience using only gold and silver coin as money, with copper change coinage rounding out the system, was disastrous—not the least because from 1789 until the late 1840's the precious metal was always in short supply. Indeed, all money was in short supply, with the various Mint officials unable to raise the requisite bonds to assume office.

The Civil War and the economic stranglehold that it created—with insufficient precious coinage to finance the struggle, let alone to fuel the economy, created a monetary crisis. Fractional pieces of paper money evolved in the interregnum. By 1863, when the Union was nearly bankrupt, Salmon P. Chase, Secretary of the Treasury, conceived the scheme for the national government to issue paper money to finance the War Between the States.

The scheme worked, but no one was sure that the Supreme Court would sustain it. When Supreme Court chief justice Roger B. Taney died, President Lincoln's choice for his successor faced two very real political issues: Was he a justice who would sustain the Emancipation Proclamation, and one who would approve of the Legal Tender Acts?

Lincoln nominated Chase, a noted abolitionist as Chief Justice, but it was not until years later that the cases came to the Supreme Court. Imagine everyone's surprise when Chase wrote the majority opinion, decided 5-4 declaring his actions as Treasury Secretary unconstitutional—and voiding legal tender notes!

Of course, that's not the end of the story. Two justices of the Supreme Court retired, President Grant named their replacements, and this time Chase was on the other side of another 5–4 decision sustaining the Legal Tender Acts, paving the way for paper money to be used much as it is today. The original legal tender notes are highly collectible. Literally, Chase's portrait appears on the $10,000 bill.

primarily as units of account in banking institutions, hence their uncirculated state. Most are available at or below the quoted prices from periodicals in the trade.

Cents, Nickels, and All the Rest

Silver may have been gone from coins for twenty-five years, but there is still a wealth of material that can be found in pocket change, ranging from the 1989 quarter without the Philadelphia Mint mark (estimated value $2 to $3 according to error collector Bill Fivaz) to a 1972 double die cent—still locatable and worth several hundred dollars—and even a 1999 wide "AM" in "America" worth hundreds of dollars.

Today, the allure of coins is different than it was a generation ago, when it was still possible to look through pocket change and regularly find coin rarities. With the removal of silver from circulating coinage, much of that mystique is gone.

A mint error of major proportion is the 1972 double die cent, manufactured at the Philadelphia Mint. The error affected fewer than 100,000 coins, most experts believe, but it makes seeing "double" worthwhile.

The reason is clear enough: as silver was removed, so too were most of the pre-1965 issues for dimes, quarters, and half dollars. The likelihood of finding *any* Mercury dime in pocket change, let alone a worn 1916-D, was severely diminished.

What has replaced this is the search through contemporary clad coinage—rolls, bags, and socks in drawers—for *any* silver coin, meaning any half dollar dated before 1970, and any dime or quarter before 1965.

Some can still be found—though increasingly, the date and condition are likely to be of minimal importance. But for the thrill of the search itself, looking for a silver coin or two can be an enjoyable way to spend a Saturday afternoon, after visiting the local bank to acquire several rolls to go through.

As to the cents and nickels, there are surely still rarities available. Wheat-backed cents, which went the way of the five-cent pay telephone call, are still found in change, and it is not unusual to look closely and find pieces from the 1920s and 30s, even if in poor condition.

The nickel circulates ubiquitously, and it is not at all unusual to find mintmarked five-centers from the 1940s, or even 1938 and 1939. They are inevitably worn and well-circulated, though somewhat valuable.

But the cents and nickels with the most value are those with mint errors—mistakes in production—that have reached the streets. A series of double dies, similar to the famous 1955, have been produced in 1972 and 1984, as well as in other years. Each is scarce and worth hundreds of dollars, even for circulated specimens. It pays therefore to continue to check your change.

Coin Grading and Prices

There's a well-recorded tale of Tom McAfee, a dealer then living in Honolulu, who made a 1969 sale of an 1883 quarter in brilliant uncirculated condition (there was no 11-point grading in those

The 1883 Hawaiian quarter had a value of $19 in 1969, more than $2,000 in 1980, and a value today of a few hundred dollars. The coin market, like many tangible assets, goes both up and down.

Portrait of a Collector

In 1997, one of the world's greatest collections of numismatic items hit the auction block. This extraordinary holding was put together over the lifetime of John Jay Pittman, the late president of the American Numismatic Association, who spent more than thirty years on the ANA board of governors.

What made it all the more remarkable was that Pittman, who died on February 17, 1996 at the age of 83, did not have the fabulous wealth of a Norweb, Eliasberg, or Garrett. He worked as a salaried employee—a chemical engineer for the Eastman Kodak Company in Rochester, New York—and bought his coins the way most collectors do: one at a time.

Over a lifetime, Pittman gathered more than 12,000 coins. Interestingly, Pittman did not have controversial coins such as an 1804 silver dollar (which was not produced by the Mint in the year it was dated) or a 1913 Liberty nickel (which was evidently manufactured by Mint employees and spirited out of the Mint). Rather, it was a collection whose early American proof gold and silver coinage was significantly more complete than that in the Smithsonian Institution's National Coin Collection, which was begun from the Mint's own cabinet.

What made the collection distinctive was its worldwide scope. Pittman was not only a master collector of American coin issues, but applied his skill and knowledge to collect rarities that rival the greatest collections of foreign coins abroad.

Japanese coins in his collection contained rarities that were in no other private collections. Many believe that only the collection of the Central Bank of Japan was better than that which Pittman collected over a lifetime. The same was true for his South African coin collection, his Cuban holdings, and even those of Hawaii.

There wasn't another collection like it—something that John Jay Pittman wasn't shy about telling others during his lifetime. He exhibited portions of his collection widely, and regularly, for others to appreciate, and to learn from.

Q. David Bowers, himself a past president of both the ANA and the Professional Numismatists Guild, spoke of the ubiquitous tools of John Jay's trained eye: "His 'trademark' was a brass-rimmed, thick-lensed magnifying glass without a handle, about half the size of a roll of silver dollars."

---

days) for $19. It was a pretty coin, but there were better ones; McAfee had uncirculated specimens for as low as $12 or $15, and for as much as $25. The coin was a nice compromise, probably an MS-63+ or MS-64. McAfee didn't grade the examples, he priced them.

In 1980, when the coin market was running amok, McAfee recalled this quarter and made a firm bid of $2,000 to re-acquire it; it wasn't for sale then. Today, the coin has a $500 value, proving that coins don't always continue to go up in value.

There are clearly other areas that can be collected relatively inexpensively. This includes rare date coinage, low mintage pieces, and (in the case of encapsulated coins), those with low slab populations (few coins encapsulated by professional grading services). One example of this is low-mintage gold coins of $5 and $10 denomination. The key is choosing well-circulated specimens.

Many pieces in fine, very fine, and xf condition, with mintages of 20,000 pieces or fewer, remain available at relatively modest prices. With gold hovering at $700 an ounce, a $10 gold piece contains .48 troy ounces of gold (about $340 worth).

For about $300 to $450 more, with little downside and a high potential upside, a circulated Carson City Mint eagle can be purchased. The series is affordable and can be acquired over a period of time, either at coin shows or through the mail.

What is surprising is how modest the price is. In fact, if someone tried to put together multiple sets, they would be virtually impossible to duplicate easily, at least insofar as acquiring multiple numbers of identical, circulated coins.

Why? Because of the high melt rate for many gold coins. And, in any event, the low mintage guarantees that there cannot be many complete sets, no matter how diligent the search for the low-mintage rarities.

Modern proof sets from 1950 also offer this as a solution to most collectors. The Mint's continuing sale of items at issue prices gives a new supply to the top end, but the complete supply at the bottom end is such that there can never be as many as 100,000 complete sets after a forty year period of time.

The Nature of Collecting

Coin collecting is fun. Coin collections can be a fun investment. That, in substance, expresses the viewpoints of dozens of dealers and collectors surveyed over the years. Harvey G. Stack, a past president of the Professional Numismatists Guild, an industry trade organization, and a dealer for more than a half century, once said that while "not every investment in coins is a collection, every collection of coins is an investment," a remark echoed by nearly everyone surveyed.

Happiness without investing in coins is still possible, and perhaps part of this is getting back to the basics that attracted people to collecting a generation or more ago: the ability to search through pocket change and find something worth more than face value.

Buyers of coins who can afford to put away their purchases and just enjoy them are often the most rewarded. That sometimes requires a strong pocketbook, and of course a desire to be a collector.

Coin collecting is what you make of it. If the collector instinct is prominent, the investor aspect may happen by itself without your even considering the implications of whether an item will or will not increase in value. Creative collecting will often lead to a solid investment in coins, even if it is not the collector's intent, a lesson that generations of coin collectors have found, often to their amazement and surprise.

CHAPTER FIVE

TOOLS OF THE COLLECTING TRADE

Coin collecting is an easy hobby that appeals to people of all ages. Of course, you can start with pocket change; but if you take the hobby seriously it won't be long before you need a means to store your collection, accoutrements to grade your coins, material to display them for your friends and family to see, and books and other research tools to learn more about your growing collection.

Storage

Let's start with the basics of coin storage. There are many alternatives at a variety of price levels. First and most importantly, you must establish whether the storage is to be part of a display, or merely removal of the coins from circulation. Next, consider the purpose of the storage and its intended location. For temporary purposes, a #6 or #10 business envelope folded over works very well. So does a plastic sandwich bag or pill tubes from a pharmacy. Of course, those are not appropriate for display or review.

For non-emergent storage, planned in advance, a 2" x 2" paper envelope holder manufac-

OPPOSITE: The GSA "mapped" a silver dollar as if it were a mountain. It shows high points that wear easily, affecting a coin's grade.

ABOVE: Placing coins in albums is a convenient way to show your collection to coin club acquaintances, friends and family. The coins are held securely in acid-free binders with a tight die-cut fit for the coin's safety. An acetate sheet slides over the coin to offer additional protection. BELOW: 2 x 2 holders are in widespread use and typically cost less than a nickel each. Use caution when stapling them together to avoid coin damage.

tured specifically to hold coins—a large-sized silver dollar is an inch and a half in diameter—is widely used in the trade. Generally, they are inexpensive, about five cents apiece, and sold in lots of 100. The envelopes are available in white, pastel colors, and manila. For long-term storage, the envelope should not contain sulphur, which can tarnish silver or interact with the copper in many cents or the copper alloy found in many gold coins. The major deficiency of the 2" x 2" paper envelope is that you have to write your description of the contents on the envelope, and can verify what's inside only by opening the envelope and removing the coin from its storage facility.

A slight upgrade is a 2" x 2" holder made of cardboard, with a hole cut and covered with an inert mylar strip. Here, the coin is placed on one side of the strip on the mylar and like a sandwich, the other side is flipped over. There are some variations on the sealing; in some cases, a self-adhesive seal puts the coin between mylar. In other cases, two or three staples are used to seal the holder. The problem with the self-adhesive is that if not carefully placed, the coin can become stuck to the glue; with staples, if the coin is misplaced, it can be damaged in the stapling process.

In conjunction with any of the 2" x 2" holders, there are inexpensive mylar shields that surround the coin like a piece of gold foiled candy. Marketed under the name Cointains®, they are typically sold in packages of twenty or twenty-five for under ten dollars.

For more expensive coins, custom holders are in widespread use; but in many instances, the holder of choice is a plastic encapsulation by a professional grading service which takes the coin (usually sent in either a cardboard-mylar holder or a paper 2" x 2" envelope), grades it, and then seals it in a plastic holder that is about 2" x 3" in size.

Holdered coins are themselves generally stored in cardboard boxes—the ones containing the unused holders work fine—or in 3" x 9" plastic versions. Typically, boxes are kept in a file cabinet, desk drawer, or safety deposit box at a bank or other financial institution. A cigar box, empty of its tobacco contents, is a useful size designed for conveniently holding many 2" x 2" envelopes.

Albums

If you decide to collect a series by date and mint-mark, or by coin design or type (a "type collection"), there are albums in a wide variety of price ranges that afford storage to the collection. Some, originally patented by Whitman in the 1930s, are die-cut into cardboard with a glued backing. A more advanced version, die-cut cardboard with mylar sleeves on both sides, allows both sides of the coin to be viewed. A typical set for say, state quarters, is available at under six dollars for uniface holders, while the dual-view holder sells in the twenty dollar range.

Square coin tubes made of inert polyethylene

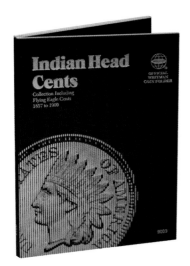 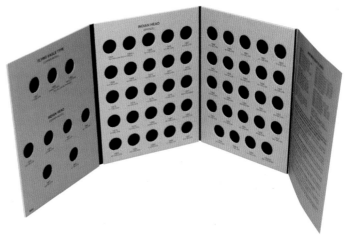

The Whitman album for Indian head cents (shown), and other coins, was invented in the 1930's by Richard Yeo. The coins are protected, but will still tarnish. This method of storage is great for circulated coins with minimal value, but probably not advised for more expensive, better-grade material.

are inexpensive and offer versatility; they are available in denominations and sizes from cent to dollar and retail for about fifty cents apiece. Polystyrene holders, also inert and free of polyvinyl chloride (PVC) that permeates some soft plastic holders, cost about seventy-five cents and can be easily viewed.

Researching a Coin

The biggest joy of being a coin collector is acquiring something new and learning about it. The internet is a great tool, as is the public library. There are thousands of books on coin collecting, and many of the ones most useful for research are in the library.

For the more advanced collector, a mail-lending library is maintained by the American Numismatic Association at its Colorado Springs headquarters. The catalogue is available for review online at www.money.org. Not available for mail delivery, but accessible at its New York headquarters in the financial district, is the library of the 150-year-old American Numismatic Society (ANS), the largest in the world and one whose librarians are always willing to assist in a research project. Their library catalogue, containing articles, books, and clippings, is also available online at www.numismatics.org.

Numismatic Literature (*NumLit*) is the annotated bibliography by the ANS of published work in all fields of numismatics, and has been issued at least twice a year since the 1940s. It covers many

The American Numismatic Association, founded in 1891, has been headquartered in Colorado Springs since 1967 on the campus of The Colorado College. It truly is the national coin club, and its headquarters is worth a detour for a memorable visit.

esoteric as well as utilitarian topics that help in any research. At its core *NumLit* is a text archive that is designed for longevity in the face of rapid technological innovation. For users, *NumLit* currently exists as subject and author indexes that are regularly updated as new titles are entered. The titles are also listed in the reverse order of when they were added. Access is through the ANS website.

Hardware

Light and magnification

Two necessary tools for viewing your coins in the best possible light (pun intended) are a light and a magnifying glass. The best lights are halogen—including flashlight versions—which bathe the coin more evenly than fluorescent or incandescent lighting does, and make grading easier because they help to bring out flaws not otherwise easily visible. A tensor-style lamp also works well. Whatever you choose should be usable in a bank safety deposit box, so if electricity is not available, batteries are essential.

A magnifying glass is also essential. First, you may need it to read date and mintmark. Second, you will need it to do fine-line grading. Two different glasses work well: a 3x or power lens gives a nice overview, and a 10–12xx magnification spots grading blemishes and wear-spots that are essential to be aware of on high-priced coins.

Examination surface

It's important that when you examine a coin, you hold or place it on or above a surface that will protect it. A rubber mat or rubberized mouse pad is useful because it can prevent damage when a coin is dropped. A thick towel will also suffice. Every experienced collector has dropped a coin now and then; make sure you're protected when it happens to you.

Surgical or latex gloves

Not something you need all the time, gloves are a great aid in handling proof coins and better-class uncirculated coins. You still should always handle a coin by its edge only—never on the surface of the obverse and reverse—because that is the least-noticed side of a coin. The gloves will prevent transfer of finger oils to any surface of a coin, important because oils will eventually etch into and permanently damage the metal.

Inventory list or program

A list of what you have collected and acquired is important, too. It keeps your collection in focus, avoids unnecessary acquisition of duplicates, and

Where to Get Your Tools

There are various sources where you can acquire the tools of the trade, ranging from magnifying glasses and holders to display stands or furniture designed to hold your coins and medals. Each has advantages and disadvantages, but all can put you in the business of collecting by this time next week.

The local coin shop can provide the basic tools and you can get a feel for how the loupe looks, handles, and works, and see if the album will fit in your safe deposit box, or is even easy to use. There is usually knowledgeable sales staff to assist.

Internet purchasing is another good choice, though it lacks immediacy and a chance to touch and feel what you are buying. Three good sources are the official website of the American Numismatic Association (www.money.org) (click tab "Shop at Money Market"); the *Numismatic News* website, www.numismatic-news.net ("Books" or "Classified Ads"); or *Coin World's* website, www.Coinworld.com ("Advertisements").

allows you to clearly set objectives for the future. There are a number of commercial checklists available, as well as computer programs advertised in many hobby periodicals. Whatever you utilize, be duplicative and back it up—even if it is a photocopy kept in another off-site place.

Consider making a photocopy of a few pages from a coin catalogue that covers your field of expertise or collecting interest. Say that you are collecting Indian head cents which were minted each year from 1859 to 1909, all of which except two were minted at the Philadelphia Mint. (Those two, by the way, are San Francisco cents of 1908 and 1909.) That takes up three or four pages in most guidebooks, but also lends itself to a spreadsheet that you can print out.

Be sure your inventory includes date and mint-mark, condition, cost, date of purchase, and source of acquisition. A space for current value is helpful. Some computerized programs and web-based sites allow this to be done easily. But avoid the temptation to log everything—it's too time consuming at first, even overwhelming—and focus instead on large areas of similarities, such as all Roosevelt dimes, type coins, and so forth.

Scale

Not essential at the start of a collecting career, a good scale is important to the experienced numismatist. Statistics are available as to weights and measures of nearly all post-medieval coins. Weight comparisons are a way to check out whether a piece is counterfeit, or if it's on the wrong size flan. For example, a Florida state quarter struck on the planchet of a nickel may look remarkably normal, but the weight difference makes the error immediately obvious.

Size matters: a Morgan (38.1 mm) dollar next to a new presidential (26.54 mm).

1999 Connecticut state quarter with cladding missing on the reverse.

Caliper

Another useful tool is a caliper, which is used to measure the width of a coin. Again, dimensions of thickness of contemporary coins are well-known, and it's an easy way to compare known statistics with the actual dimensions. Thin or thick planchets are error coins that have a value exceeding typical coins. A state quarter without a level of cladding—the white bread sandwich part of the modern quarters, not the copper "meat"— routinely sells in the secondary market for $300 or more and is detectable on sight, weight, and by careful checking with a tool.

A caliper can also be used as a substitute for a ruler, although if used as such should be in millimeters, not inches. For sizes under three inches, most numismatic dimensions are given in millimeters (mm). It is not uncommon for a serious collector to be accurate in size estimation to two millimeters. By way of example, a golden presidential dollar is 26.5 mm in size, while a Morgan silver dollar is 38.1 mm.

Size is important for another reason. There are some coins from bygone eras that are substantially identical in design, but not size. The caliper or ruler helps you identify which coin is which. The $2.50 quarter eagle minted from 1796 to 1807 is 20 mm in size. It has no denomination associated with it, a fact that changed in 1808. It is similar to the 1797–1804 $10 eagle, 33 mm in size, also with no denomination visible.

Coin Clubs

Novice collectors should seriously consider joining a coin collector's club. In the club environment, more experienced collectors can show a new collector how to use the tools of the trade to better enjoy the world's most fascinating hobby. Clubs meet in many different locations and come in all shapes and sizes; some larger corporations will have a hobby club that meets after hours or during lunch, and many adult education programs sponsor coin clubs. Local churches seeking a little extra money from renting out a room once a month are another frequent location for a local coin club. There is no definitive listing, but more than 500 clubs are members of the American Numismatic Association, which is billed as America's coin club.

Just 4,146 quarter eagles were minted in 1796. Note the "puny eagle" on the reverse holding an olive wreath. The following year (1797) a heraldic eagle would be introduced, his beak turned ominously toward arrows of war.

The 1804 eagle or $10 gold piece was not a coin of the people; only 3,757 were coined at the Philadelphia Mint. The attractive design has an unusual and sometimes overlooked feature on the reverse: the eagle's beak reflects the militancy of the young American nation, poised for war with the head pointed towards the arrows in its talons.

Specialty coin collecting societies allow those who share common specialties to share their experiences and common interests. One of the oldest groups is the Token & Medal Society (TAMS), founded more than forty years ago as a haven for those who collect medallions, tokens, and other cash substitutes. Around a thousand dedicated members are involved in the organization, which meets once each year as part of the American Numismatic Association's annual convention, the world's largest coin show.

Most local groups cross-pollinate with state and regional organizations, and addresses change frequently as officers rotate. For instance, the Border Town Coin Club (www.bordertowncoinclub.org) of Fort Smith, Arkansas meets monthly and sponsors an annual spring show over a three-day weekend. The club is affiliated with the Arkansas Numismatic Society and Oklahoma Numismatic Association.

A "Show Directory" appears in *Numismatic News* on a weekly basis; *Coin World* has a weekly "Show Calendar" that conveniently marks clubs, and the American Numismatic Association website has a club listing (www.money.org), and allows searches by collecting topic and even by zip code. *Numismatic News* has an annual calendar listing of coin shows and club meetings on its website (www.numismaticnews.net), and *Coin World*'s paid online subscription (www.Coinworld online.com) also lists shows and club meetings.

Clubs have many educational components. There are usually speakers at each meeting, a version of show and tell on either new acquisitions or topics of the evening, and a lot of camaraderie. A mini-course usually takes place either at the start of the evening or during an intermission where collectors and vest-pocket dealers sell their duplicates, or trade items with their colleagues and fellow collectors.

Attending coin shows

Most states have organizations that hold shows or conventions at least annually. There are also regional groups, such as the Central States Numismatic Society or the New England Numismatic Association, which may hold larger regional shows.

Large educational shows with fixed dates include FUN (Florida United Numismatists), held in January since 1955 and July since 2007, the Michigan State Numismatic Association annual convention over Thanksgiving weekend. There are also large commercial shows such as the one at Long Beach,

California, held three times a year in February, June, and October. All offer educational opportunities as well as a chance to buy items on your want list.

Exhibiting Your Coin Collection

One of the most fun and exciting things about collecting is showing off your collection. You can do that with friends and family in an informal way, or display it at a convention where educational exhibits are welcomed.

Standard sized "All State" display cases common to the jewelry and collectibles field work fairly well. They have the benefit of being lockable to prevent petty theft.

Most organizations that encourage competitive exhibits have rules. A common error of a novice exhibitor is titling the exhibit improperly, meaning that the caption is not related to the numismatic material. Judges decide which display wins best in category and best in show.

In preparing an exhibit, background is as important as foreground, and preventing coin damage is essential. Velvet works as an effective cushion and attractive background. A flair for the artistic helps.

One way to see what makes a great display is to visit a museum with numismatic holdings and see how they do it.

Popper was a Romanian national who struck his own gold coinage in Argentina by weight in the 1880s. That was typical of many pioneer-types who made their own coinage which went on to local acceptance and latter-day collecting.

Celebrating the statehood of Hawaii in 1959 is this official medal. Medal collecting is widespread since the time of Pisaniello. Unlike coins, medals have no face value.

Coin (Numismatic) Museums

There are museums that specialize in numismatic items, such as The American Numismatic Society (96 Fulton Street, New York City), located in downtown New York City. The ANS, organized in 1858, operates as a research museum. The original objectives of the ANS, "the collection and preservation of coins and medals, the investigation of matters connected therewith, and the popularization of the science of Numismatics," have evolved into a more modern mission statement: "The mission of the ANS is to be the pre-eminent national institution advancing the study and appreciation of coins, medals, and related objects of all cultures as historical and artistic documents, by maintaining the foremost numismatic collection and library, by supporting scholarly research and publications, and by sponsoring educational and interpretive programs for diverse audiences."

Featuring Fakes

The seriousness of modern numismatic counterfeiting can be gleaned from the pages of *The Numismatist*, the monthly journal of the American Numismatic Association (ANA) which, starting in 1966, ran a regular column entitled "Featuring Fakes" by ANA member Virgil Hancock.

Hancock championed the creation of the American Numismatic Authentication Trust (ANAT) which was the predecessor of the ANA Certification service (ANACS). The original purpose of ANACS was not to be the grading guardian that it later became, but rather to be a first-class laboratory and diagnostician of counterfeit coins—one readily available to the masses.

Prior to that time, the only reliable methods of authenticating a coin were either to show it to a dealer who was skilled in a particular area, or to send it to the Mint laboratory in Washington for review. When coin dealers A-Mark asked the Secret Service for assistance with an 1893-S dollar, the government damaged the coin and then refused any compensation. A-Mark sued, and lost.

Mint technicians were useful within limitations, but the anti-counterfeiting laws (for regular issue coinage) theoretically precluded them from returning coins that were thought not to be genuine.

Finally, Hancock and others, got behind the efforts to create an authentication service that would be based in Washington so that it could use the Mint and Smithsonian reference collections; ANACS was born. And ANACS proved to be necessary, because many international coin duplicators began moving from counterfeiting $20 gold pieces to many counterfeiting rarities. As of June 15, 1972, the contribution of nearly 900 hobbyists and 247 coin clubs made the establishment of ANACS a reality.

Other Museums

Some selected museums with extensive numismatic displays include

Judah L. Magnes Museum, Berkeley, CA (Jewish American Hall of Fame medal series, ancient and modern foreign coinage)

Bank of California Money Museum, San Francisco, CA (Wells Fargo & Co., American and foreign coins)

Museum of Connecticut History, Hartford, CT (Mitchelson collection of U.S. coins and medals)

Mystic Seaport Museum, Mystic, CT (U.S. and foreign coins and paper money)

Delaware State Museum, Dover, DE (numismatic items)

Mel Fisher Maritime Museum, Key West, FL (Spanish treasure ship coinage)

Field Museum of Natural History, Chicago, IL (numismatic items)

Indiana University Art Museum, Bloomington, IN (Ancient Greek, Roman, and Byzantine coinage)

Notre Dame Gore Memorial coin and currency collection at the Hesburgh Library, Notre Dame, IN

Museum of Fine Arts, Boston, MA (ancient coins, medals)

Peabody Museum of Salem, Salem, MA (numismatic items)

Eric P. Newman Money Museum at Washington University, St. Louis, MO (numismatic items and books)

University of North Carolina, Wilson Library at Chapel Hill, NC (colonial coinage and paper money)

Newark Museum, Newark, NJ (numismatic items and library)

Princeton University Numismatic Collection at Firestone Library, Princeton, NJ (extensive ancient collection and other numismatic items)

Ashland University Numismatic Center, Ashland, OH, Cleveland Museum of Art, Cleveland, OH (R. Henry Norweb British gold in collection),

Carnegie Museum, Pittsburgh, PA (numismatic items)

Banco Popular de Puerto Rico Numismatic Collection, Old San Juan Branch, San Juan, PR

Texas Memorial Museum, Austin, TX (Swanson collection of numismatic items)

Federal Reserve Bank of New York, New York, NY (exhibit of American numismatic history on loan from American Numismatic Society)

Federal Reserve Bank of Richmond, Richmond, VA (American money)

West Virginia State Museum, Charleston, WV (numismatic items)

State Historical Society, Madison, WI (American numismatics)

You may also want to check out the library and online coin cabinet of the American Numismatic Society (www.numismatics.org), the library and virtual museum of the American Numismatic Association (www. money.org), or the virtual museum of The National Numismatic Collection, (http://american history.si.edu/collections/numismatics).

A number of museums and private collectors maintain websites. Most notable is the Harry W. Bass, Jr. Foundation Numismatic Index to Periodicals (NIP): www.harrybassfoundation.org/links.htm. Links to the extended collection are also available.

The ANS numismatic collection, estimated at approximately 800,000 coins and related objects, is rivaled only by the largest state collections of Europe. ANS cabinets are particularly strong in Ancient Greek coins; Roman Republican coinage; Islamic, Chinese, Latin American, and United States coinage—both the Colonial series and Federal issues; as well as in private coinages.

The ANS has on view at the Federal Reserve Bank of New York an exhibit called "Drachmas,

BELOW: Falkland Island coinage that cannot be used in Argentina (they call it the Malvinas) and bears the portrait of the British sovereign, here Queen Elizabeth II. The British at nearby Port Lockroy base in Antarctica accept no Argentina currency, a vestige of the war in the 1980s.

Doubloons, and Dollars: The History of Money" which includes over 800 examples of the Society's noted collection including the Brasher doubloon, the 1804 dollar, the Confederate States half-dollar, and the world's most valuable coin, the 1933 Double Eagle (on loan).

The museum of the American Numismatic Association (818 North Cascade Ave., Colorado Springs, CO) consists of over 250,000 objects encompassing the history of numismatics, from the earliest invention of money to the present day. The collection includes paper money, coins, tokens, medals, and traditional money from all over the world. Highlights from the collection include individual rarities such as the 1804 dollar, the 1913 Liberty head nickel, and the Aubrey E. and Adeline I. Bebee collection of United States paper money.

RIGHT: Harry W. Bass was an outstanding collector, a longtime member of the American Numismatic Association, and a past president of the American Numismatic Society. The Bass Foundation established both a virtual museum (online) and a gallery at the American Numismatic Association Museum in Colorado Springs, Colorado, that is exquisite in its presentation of portions of the collection Bass acquired during his lifetime.

CHAPTER SIX

FINDING COINS FOR YOUR COLLECTION

Coin collecting is not an inexpensive hobby, except at its most basic level—such as putting together a collection of Lincoln Memorial cents from circulation, where fifty years' worth of coinage only requires a cash investment of two dollars or so. But to complete a set, most collectors will have to include some coins unlikely to be found in circulation, plus proof coins intended to be sold to collectors; these proof cents were made annually from 1959–1964 and 1968–2007 (No proof coins were minted in the 1965–1967 period because of a national coin shortage). A complete set also generally includes some key error coins: the 1960-D large date cut over small date; a 1970-S small date (high 7); 1971-S double die; 1972 double die; 1984 double die; 1990 proof (no "S"); 1992-D (close "AM" in "America"); 1995 double die; and 1999 wide "AM" in "America." Such error coins can easily add $9,000 to the face value price tag.

For higher denominations, particularly those made of precious metal, there are two components to consider: the face value and the metal content. For example, if you wanted to collect double eagle $20 gold coins from the first year of issue (1849) to the design change of 1877, there are over eighty different dates and mintmarks involved. The face value alone is $1,600; the

OPPOSITE: Bicentennial quarter.

1946 War Nickel Found in Pocket Change

A 1946 silver composition "war nickel" was found in pocket change in the San Francisco Bay Area, authenticated, and encapsulated by the Professional Coin Grading Service (PCGS) with a grade of fine-12 on the 1 to 70 Sheldon grading scale. Burton Blumert of Camino Coin Co. in Burlingame, California, reported the discovery. He says that a dealer friend, Carter Collins of Collectible Coins in Mill Valley, California, was searching through a coffee can full of war nickels to fill a client's order when he saw the unusual coin that had the right color, wear, and style—but the "wrong" date.

Collins brought the oddity to Blumert, who was convinced it was genuine, but wanted further confirmation. He in turn asked well-known error specialist Fred Weinberg to examine the coin. After a brief look-see, Weinberg was also convinced—and made the recommendation that the coin be encapsulated by the PCGS.

The coin is in a strong fine condition—well worn, from a lifetime of circulation, but nonetheless bearing that unique silver-gray color that is the hallmark of war nickels. War nickels were authorized by Congress on March 27, 1942 to take the place of the copper/nickel five-cent coin because copper and nickel were both critical war materials used for munitions. The coin's composition before the war was 25 percent nickel, 75 percent copper.

With nickel and copper in short supply, the copper cent was eliminated (a steel substitute was supplied), a three-cent piece authorized (but never produced), and a composition change made consisting of 35 percent silver, 56 percent copper, and 9 percent manganese. To further distinguish the coins, and to allow for their eventual withdrawal from circulation, large mintmarks P, D, and S were placed above the Monticello dome on the reverse.

Approximately 870 million war nickels were produced from 1942 to 1945, using about fifty million ounces of silver from the strategic reserve. (That same reserve was utilized until just recently to produce American bullion eagle coins.)

Off-metal error coins are more common than generally believed, but a 1946 silver-planchet war nickel is a significant rarity. In *Walter Breen's Complete Encyclopedia of U.S. Coins* (1988), Breen catalogues it as #2703 and refers to it as "extremely rare." He notes "at least 4 authenticated to date," all of which, like this one, are from the Philadelphia Mint.

Unlike some modern error coins or even the 1933 double eagles that have been pursued by government authorities, the fine-12 condition of this one makes clear that this coin had a long life in circulation, and was evidently put there via the proper channels.

Though precisely how the error was produced is unknown, it is probable that there were blank planchets from 1946 that were simply tossed into the production hopper—and then struck into coin in 1946, where as a shiny, new, uncirculated piece, it looked remarkably like the nickel-copper coins otherwise produced in that year.

It also shows that error coins are still out there, undiscovered, years after they were produced and entered circulation—and that a coin doesn't have to be in top uncirculated condition in order to command a significant price premium.

If there's a hint from this, it might well be that the "junk box" in your local coin dealer's store could have a treasure trove for the looking—if you take the time, do the research, and look at the coins.

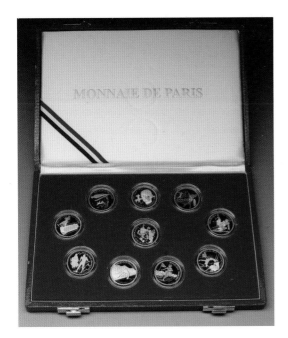

Ten Piece French Gold Proof Set commemorating the Albertville Olympics.

One of the recent varieties that is highly collectible is the 1992-D cent close AM in America. The "Wide AM" in America, 1998 and 1999, is a recent error on Lincoln cents. Lettering is still cut in by hand as it was when the Mint started in 1792, so errors or visual discrepancies happen occasionally.

San Francisco mints), and the 1870-CC Carson City mint double eagle.

If there is a common denominator in older rarities, and the mint responsible for the errors, it is the historic old mint at Carson City, Nevada, which functioned from 1870 until 1889. The 1870-CC $20, from the first year of issue, is a key rarity.

bullion content is over $50,000—before even considering rarity factors. (The 1849 $20 is a rare pattern; the unique example is in the Smithsonian National Coin Collection.) Other rarities include the 1861 Paquet reverse (from the Philadelphia and

This is an 1883-S double eagle or $20 gold piece. Containing nearly an ounce of gold, bulk quantities of double eagles were shipped abroad to settle trade debts and international balance of payments obligations.

Double eagle production started with this 1849 $20 pattern unique. Regular production began in 1850 and continued until 1933. Later, millions of double eagles were melted at FDR's direction.

Grading the 1870-CC Double Eagle

Disagreements on grading rarities, or even regular coins, are not that uncommon. Over a few years, three major dealers—Paramount, Superior, and Stack's—all sold the same 1870-CC double eagle, which each agreed was the finest known, except that Stack's called it about uncirculated (AU), Superior termed it XF-45, and Paramount thought to be XF-40.

The coin had not changed condition in between; the order of auction showed it went to Stack's as AU (equivalent, say, to 55), then to Superior (45), Paramount (40), and then back to Stack's who stuck with their original about uncirculated grade. (Upon viewing the coin, Bob Arnel—a New York and later North Carolina collector who made something of a specialty of Carson City Mint coinage—commented that he thought it was simply "struck circulated" by the Mint, meaning that the coin was uncirculated, but looked worn.)

Rarest of the Carson City dollars is this 1870-cc $20 NGC AU-50. Some say the coining conditions were so primitive all of the double eagles were struck "circulated." This coin is one of the best grades known.

Pocket Change

If you haven't been checking your pocket change, or the junk box in your local dealer's store, or even the mystery box of unsorted coins at the local coin show at the Legion Hall, you could be missing the boat.

With more than 125 billion clad coins produced by the U.S. Mint in the last forty-five years, the product of the Coinage Act of 1965 has gone on, to the surprise of almost everyone, to be one of the grandest and most successful experiments ever to result from a failure.

Today, more than forty years after the inflationary trend ended precious metal coinage, and a quarter century after the coin shortages of the mid-1960s, the ten and twenty-five cent denominations are circulating freely. Silver has been removed almost entirely from circulating coinage. The quarter dollars created for the Bicentennial were originally expected to cause production problems, but efficient manufacturing and distribution minimized potential shortages during issuance in 1975 and 1976. Indeed, this set the stage for the successful state quarter clad program that began in 1999. Highly collectible (the state quarter clad program has singlehandedly created a whole new generation of coin collectors), there are some rarities in the clad issues taken just from circulation. Examples

1776–1976 dated bicentennial quarter, struck from mid-1975 until January, 1977. The person responsible for Congress agreeing to issue this coin, which the Mint opposed, was John Jay Pittman, then ANA President.

1982 no mintmark dime. The coin is a circulation strike that omits any mintmark, an error making pocket change searches worthwhile. At that time, mintmarks were added by hand-punching the dies, and the technician omitted this crucial step.

include the 1982 no mintmark dime; errors in the state quarter series that sell for thousands of dollars; a 1974-D double die half dollar; and some low-mintage proof pieces such as the 1981-S (clear S) Susan B. Anthony dollar. State quarter errors, including the recent Wisconsin issue, are available at 25 cents apiece from pocket change but could someday be worth much more.

Designs also include the special Bicentennial commemorative quarter, half and dollar, which include the silver-clad issues with .074 troy ounces of the precious metal for the quarter and in multiples for the half and dollar. Collecting clads is now a substantial undertaking, in part because of the state quarter design additions which have already added half of the 50 states, and contain mintmarks

from Philadelphia, Denver, and San Francisco mints. But it is still an affordable and fun way to collect coins of the modern era.

Bulk Acquisition from Banks

Finding uncirculated coins in pocket change or at face value cost is a painstaking process, but is still doable. This involves bulk buying of coins, soon to become more difficult as the Mint goes to larger-quantity bags. The aim is to avoid coins with any evidence of wear on the surface.

One problem in acquiring a coin free of surface mars or scratches is that the speed that the Mint requires—a new design processed every ten weeks—makes the production process sloppy.

Wisconsin state quarter error. The coin is an error worth far more than face value, due to a manufacturing error in the depiction of the corn. There are several different varieties.

Errors in the state quarter program make checking pocket change important. The coins can have a variety of visually obvious mistakes that include clips, double and triple strikes, and even the wrong size planchet or metal composition. All are highly collectible.

Buying Coins Directly from the Mint

You can buy coins directly from many mints, including the U.S. Mint. Get on their mailing list either through an internet site or via postage-paid mail. Most mints prefer the internet because they can avoid prohibitive postage costs.

Here are some mints that have interesting products, and whose mailing lists you may wish to join:

U.S. Mint
801 9th Street, NW
Washington, DC 20220 USA
www.usmint.gov

The Royal Mint (UK)
14101 Southcross Drive West
Burnsville, MN 55337 USA
Tel: 1-800-517-6468
www.royalmint.com

La Monnaie de Paris (France)
11, quai de Conti
75270 Paris Cedex 06, France
Tel: 01-40-46-56-66
www.monnaiedeparis.com

Ufficio Filatelico e Numismatico (Vatican City)
Governatorato
00120 Città del Vaticano, Vatican City
Tel: 0039-06-6988-3708
www.vatican.va/vatican_city_state/services/stamps_coins/index_it.htm

Instituto Poligrapfico e Zecca dello Stato (Italy)
Via Gino Capponi, 47/49
00179 Roma, Italy
Tel: +39-06-85081
www.ipzs.it

Real Casa de la Moneda (Spain)
Fabrica Nacional de Moneda y Timbre
C/ Jorge Juan, 106
28071 Madrid, Spain
Tel: +34-91-566-66-66
www.fnmt.es/en/html/ho-ho.asp

Koninklijke Nederlandse Munt (Netherlands)
Postbus 2407
3500 GK, Utrecht, Netherlands
Tel: +31 -30-2910465
http://nl.knm.nl

Japan Mint (Japan)
Temma 1-chome
Kita-ku, Osaka 530-0043, Japan
Tel: +81-6-6351-5087
www.mint.go.jp

Royal Australian Mint (Australia)
Denison St
Deakin ACT 2600, Australia
Tel: +61-2-6202-6800
www.ramint.gov.au

Royal Canadian Mint (Canada)
320 Sussex Drive
Ottawa, ON K1A 0G8, Canada
Tel: (613) 993-8990
www.mint.ca

Swissmint (Switzerland)
Bernastrasse 28
CH-3003 Bern, Switzerland
Tel: +41 (0)31 322 60 68
www.swissmint.ch

NY State quarter, PCGS MS-66. Note that across the center-line of the state is an addition that goes to right angles: the Erie Canal, which was added to the original design at the insistence of Governor George Pataki.

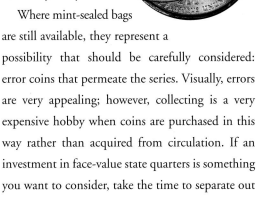

Sometimes, the coins have a lower than usual relief meaning the surface picks up flaws very easily.

Where mint-sealed bags are still available, they represent a possibility that should be carefully considered: error coins that permeate the series. Visually, errors are very appealing; however, collecting is a very expensive hobby when coins are purchased in this way rather than acquired from circulation. If an investment in face-value state quarters is something you want to consider, take the time to separate out the higher-graded coins.

You'll quickly become experienced in picking out which are the "best" graded after you've looked at five thousand Massachusetts quarters or North Carolina or Vermont designs. Then, think about having some of them encapsulated to try and reach the ethereal MS-67 or above. A New York (Denver Mint) in MS-67 has a value of $200—so even with a $15 encapsulation charge, that gives you the potential of a return of over 1,200 percent in a short period of time.

Some of the other dates have an equally brilliant (uncirculated) past—and may have a bright future.

But that will involve finding them, one by one, out of your pocket change, making your bank a partner in collecting.

Junk Boxes

The "junk box" at a local coin show, street fair, or antique shop could have a treasure trove for the looking—if you take the time, do the research, and look at the coins. Error coins, where big money can be made from pocket change, include many of relatively modern and recent vintage, such as from the state quarter program. Because of the rush to produce so many, there are "off center" types that are modest, but visible, that have a resale value of a few dollars apiece, as well as multi-struck pieces that sell in the hundreds of dollars.

Of course there are still silver coins to be found in change. They're worth at least eight times face value. All dimes and quarters of this type date prior to 1965, when the Coinage Act replaced them with copper-nickel. Half dollars in this grouping were made of forty percent silver from 1965–1970 and are also still around; the earlier ones are 90 percent silver. A pre-1965 half dollar has almost five dollars' worth of silver in it; a 1965–1970s half dollar's precious metal worth is almost two dollars.

It's a myth that dealers cherry-pick through junk boxes or even coffee cans full of coins that they acquire. One reason is the sheer time that's involved—and the energy to catalogue them. Nearly thirty years ago, when the price of silver rose to $48 an ounce, dealers were taking in millions of dollars worth of silver coins each day and melting them down without a second thought.

(The 1964 quarter in uncirculated condition had a "melt" value of nine dollars or more per coin, and few thought those price levels could be achieved again.)

At Coen-Messer Coin Co. in New York City, armored cars pulled onto the sidewalk and bags of silver coins piled on the floor of the store were literally thrown in—moving in and out at such a rate that there was little time to keep track of dates and mintmarks.

At annual American Numismatic Association conventions, many dealers will sell unsorted boxes of material at a fixed price. To the knowledgeable collector, this can be both a treat and a highly profitable venture.

Your Local Bank

Another great source for building collections is your local bank. Go to the teller with a $20 bill and ask for change. That could be eighty quarters (two rolls), four rolls of dimes (200 in total), ten rolls of nickels (400 coins) or forty rolls of cents, each containing fifty coins. Then take them home and really *look* at the coins. You can try and sort the coins by date and mintmark, or by grade, as it's easy to separate and grade when you have a large number of coins to compare. Chances are good that you may spot a minor mint error, or something that is worth more than face value. If you have a coin album for the series you are examining, it won't be long before it's half full. The second half is tougher, and generally involves more trips to the bank—or a greater initial capitalization.

Some banks have installed counting machines that allow you to simply deposit loose change and to then get a credit that you can exchange with the teller, or deposit directly into your account. In New York, New Jersey, and Pennsylvania, Commerce Bank pioneered that program, which is mutually beneficial. You get a place to easily exchange coins, and the bank saves delivery and quantity charges from the Federal Reserve Bank. That's right, for your local bank to give you a roll of pennies costs the bank more than fifty cents!

This also is the reason for the success of Coinstar, whose ubiquitous machines—more than

A 2007 issue presidential coin error: The middle coin is missing the national motto on its rim.

65,000 nationwide—now recirculate more coins each year than the U.S. Mint produces, about sixteen billion strong.

Coins of the Byzantine Empire (now modern-day Turkey) are found in many museums and markets. The American Numismatic Society in New York has a particularly fine collection.

Local Merchants

Another source for collecting circulating coins is the cash drawers of local merchants. When you do business with them on a regular basis, they frequently will exchange twenty quarters in their register for a five dollar bill. When you tell the cashier that you're a coin collector, you can probably enlist their help in locating a state quarter design your collection is missing, or even more.

Cashiers in fast food restaurants that you frequent are another source; if you buy a hamburger or combination and pay with a higher denomination bill, you can always ask to be paid in register change. If you feel funny saying it's for your coin collection, you can always use the parking meter or highway toll ploy.

Once again, it is helpful to deposit the coins into one or more albums, a good way to measure partial completion of a project as well as to separate more valuable coins from common varieties.

Travel

If you are fortunate enough to travel, you can substantially build up your numismatic acquisitions. "D" and older non-proof "S" mintmarks increase exponentially in circulation change west of the Mississippi River. "P" mintmarks prevail in the eastern United States. You won't find an "O" in New Orleans anymore, a "C" in Chalotte, or a "CC" in Carson City. Those mints are long gone.

International travel affords an entirely different opportunity: to see coin museums the world over as well as to acquire local currency and coin that forms a nice type collection, complete by design but not date and mintmark. You can also "travel" through the pages of numismatic periodicals where the only limitation on coins you acquire is your financial circumstances.

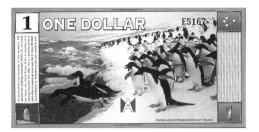

Pseudo currency of Antarctica bought at Port Lockroy, Antarctica, by the author in January, 2005, during the Austral summer. Antarctica has no real currency of its own and has a seasonal population of scientists and a few visiting tourists who use a mélange of international currencies to buy souvenirs.

Antarctica

It's the fifth largest continent in terms of area and has the smallest population. A total summer population of 4,000 shrinks to a quarter of that size in winter. Its land mass is regulated by twenty-seven consultative nations and eighteen non-consultative nations, all of whom have signed an international treaty.

Australia, Chile, and Argentina claim Antarctica as being in their exclusive economic zones (EEZ), but at least seven other nations have conflicting and overlapping claims that affect everything from the money used by tourists to pay for goods, to who is given permission to land on the barren rocks (inhabited typically with more penguins and seals than people). Fishing is one of its major industries. Tourism is the other, though only about 13,000 tourists visited in 2006—using a melange of collectible currencies to settle their bills at trading posts and research stations.

Welcome to Antarctica, the forbidding southern continent. Larger than Australia or continental Europe, with scientific research stations and remnants of whaling and a colonial past on its barren land surface, 98 percent of the mass is ice and snow. The balance is barren rock.

Tourism in Antarctica is unique because while there are "cities" in the form of research stations and abandoned whale oil factories to visit, traditional infrastructure is almost entirely lacking. Typically, visitors are attracted to exquisite scenery and wildlife.

Visits to Antarctica generally require a two-day sail across the Drake Passage, reputedly the roughest waters in the world. The trip from Ushuaia, whether aboard a small boat or a large cruise ship, is seldom calm because of the confluence of the Atlantic, Pacific, and the Antarctic Oceans.

Argentina's polar region includes Antarctica, the Malvinas (Falkland Islands), and Tierra del Fuego province. Its Antarctic currency has a history all its own, none of which is more fascinating than the gold coinage of Julius Popper, a Romanian national who settled in Ushuaia and minted his own gold coins in 1 gram and 5 gram weights. (At 36.5 mm in diameter, the 5 gram coin is nearly the size of a silver dollar).

A visit to Port Lockroy and nearby Cuverville Island involves an anchorage used by whalers and established by the British in 1944 to monitor German wartime shipping activities. At the Port Lockroy trading hut, visitors can buy postage stamps at the royal post office and put mail into the familiar red crown-sealed royal mail box. The gift and boutique shop takes U.S., U.K., and euro coins and currency, but not Argentinian money. The Falkland Islands war is still being fought.

To pay for our $89 purchase, $90 cash was tendered. Received as change: 50 pence UK dated 2004 (newly minted) with a current portrait of Queen Elizabeth; a 2 pence coin (1992) from the Falkland Islands, a 1p uncirculated coin from Falkland Islands dated 1998 (which has a penguin reverse—very appropriate); a 2 cent euro (2003), a 10 eurocent (1999), and a 5 pence UK (2004). The Commonwealth is alive and well.

On another day, more touring by small boat, this time to the large U.S. research facility called Palmer Station, one of three in Antarctica. The Palmer Long-Term Ecological Research (LTER) study area is located to the west of the Antarctic Peninsula extending south and north of the Palmer Basin from onshore to several hundred kilometers offshore. Palmer Station, on Anvers Island midway down the Antarctic Peninsula, is one of the three U.S. research stations located in Antarctica.

Passports are stamped USA-Antarctica. The station has a store—for tee-shirt and sweatshirt purchases—and, incredibly, some Antarctic money, a paper pseudo-currency by a Washington state firm in $1 denomination that is sold for face value and quite colorfully engraved with penguins and wildlife. (Everything here is penguins!) The notes are redeemable in Washington state by mail for face value until 2008. Featured design: diving Adelie Penguins on Paulet Island. The flip side of the note shows vivid, scenic, barren Antarctica. (The Antarctica Overseas Exchange Office Ltd., of Custer, Washington, has issued them.) One Antarctican dollar is equivalent to $1 U.S. The notes are not legal tender in the Antarctic—that is, there is no compulsory acceptance—but the notes may be used there if the giver and the receiver agree.

The Internet

No event or method has had more impact on collecting than the internet. Today you can find the population of encapsulated (graded) coins online (www.pcgs.com; www.ngccoin.com), read about what happened in rare coin news (www.coinworldonline.com; www.numismaticnews.com), and buy coins on eBay (www.ebay.com), or from advertisements on the *Coin World* or Numismatic News websites.

You can find out how the Coinage Act of 1873 passed congress (http://thomas.loc.gov) or search for just about anything relating to numismatics (www.google.com). Many coin clubs have websites, easily locatable through the ANA website (www.money.org); some dealer organizations also list their memberships (www.pngdealers.com). The internet has already revolutionized numismatic research and pricing in the marketplace, and it is expected to do more in years to come.

To Learn More

It's hard to predict what results you can expect from searching pocket change, or from a junk box. It depends on your level of skill and memory retention. Before you get started, however, it's worthwhile to pass along a comment made by the late Aaron Feldman, a New York City dealer whose small Sixth

1923-S Peace dollar, a common date with more than 19 million pieces minted. Millions of silver dollars were melted through the years, often to take advantage of a law passed by Congress that allowed the bullion to be re-struck into new silver dollar coinage.

Avenue shop had a simple placard: "Buy the Book Before the Coin."

Books can teach you how to grade (on-the-job training is a good substitute), can show you how to spot minor mint errors your untutored eyes might otherwise miss, can advise you of the value of certain dates and mintmarks, and can provide you with the useful starting point of mintages.

More advanced texts can even offer the number of encapsulated coins in a particular grade by a grading service. That's something worthy of reminder. Take a 1923-S Peace silver dollar (19 million pieces minted at San Francisco). The *NumisMedia* price guide lists the coin in very fine condition at around $14, the same as 1922 (51 million pieces minted), 1922-D (15 million), 1922-S (17 million) and 1925 (10 million). In Mint State 65 and Mint State 66, the prices are quoted together with the number of PCGS pieces so encapsulated (see box below).

Date	Mintage	VF20	MS60	MS65	MS66	PCGS-60	PCGS-65	PCGS-66
1922-P	51	$14	$18	$170	$730	64	4,362	413
1922-D	15	$14	$25	$355	$1,840	42	960	133
1922-S	17	$14	$20	$2,280	$8,810	49	207	6
1923-S	19	$14	$26	$5,690	$20,000	49	93	2
1925-P	10	$14	$18	$175	$740	56	5,268	1,162

Note: Mintage in millions, prices in dollars. Number encapsulated by condition. Prices per *NumisMedia*, March, 2007. PCGS population as of March, 2007.

CHAPTER SEVEN

WHAT'S IT WORTH?

Peole collect coins for many different reasons, but the storehouse of value that each contains ranks high with nearly every collector. It starts with the young child who finds an Indian head cent in pocket change (face value, 1¢) and discovers that the coin can be sold for $2.50. A more experienced collector views a coin in a dealer's case, sees the price, and recognizes a bargain. Another collector attends a public auction and successfully bids while a serious competitor is outside on a cigarette break.

In other words, there are any number of factors that affect both a coin's value and a collector's ability to acquire it. Luck is not a bad way to start.

It's hard for a novice to understand how a coin in truly crummy condition (that's not a numismatic term, but you know it when you see it) can be worth tens of thousands of dollars, and a new, shiny coin can be worth only face value. But a poor-1 graded coin (on a 1 to 70 scale, with 1 being the worst) can still have substantial value, based on other factors.

There are at least a half dozen factors that affect the value of a coin, and each works independently of the others as well as collectively. Interestingly, the conclusions can be contradictory

OPPOSITE: A liberty seated quarter, minted in 1872, now in "very fine" condition.

An 1804 dollar, type III, made in the 1850s. All of the coins were manufactured in a year other than the official date on the coin. The Mint records showing 19,000 pieces coined are simply inaccurate.

and even counterintuitive. For example, a coin with a high mintage might be very common, but if few exist in better grade condition, the better grade coin might be very valuable. Similarly, a low-mintage coin has the potential for substantial value, but that may be diminished by the existence of many examples in superior graded condition.

Quantities Minted

For modern coins, the Mint has been reluctant to release mintage quantity statistics, particularly for commemorative coins. For older coins, there are a number of sources. Official government documents are not the best source, though; among early Mint records, particularly during its first half century, there are numerous mistakes. Annual reports of the Director of the Mint, for example, tell

$1 gold pieces were struck from 1849 to 1889. Their theoretical value was that of a silver dollar, but they bought more than their silver counterpart. In fact, stores frequently posted prices on items for sale in gold, silver, and paper. Each was different. It made shopping a challenge.

The eagle or $10 gold piece was produced between 1795 and 1933, plus some modern commemorative issues. Its weight is around a half ounce of gold (0.48 troy ounces).

us that in 1804, 19,000 silver dollars were produced. But in fact, it is probable that there were *no* silver dollars manufactured that year, at least none with an 1804 date. They were all produced at a later time, but based on the erroneous Mint records, people thought they were made in the year dated.

Besides the government books' inaccuracy, there is another depleting factor: melting. As many as one-third of all the gold coins ever manufactured were melted after the great gold recall of 1933. Thus, lists of mintage statistics of these coins are widely inaccurate. Millions of silver dollars also ended up in the government's melting cauldrons following World War I, and in the 1960s millions of silver coins were destroyed for their metal content.

$5 gold pieces began production in 1795 and ended general circulation in 1929. Containing roughly a quarter ounce of gold, the coin was a workhorse of the economy. Commemorative gold coins still bear the denomination today.

Here's a brief summary of what the government melted down:

Denomination	Total minted to 1970	Total melted to 1970	% of total mintage melted
Large cent (prior to 1857)	156.2	1.308	0.84%
Flying eagle cent (1857–58)	158.7	7.469	4.71%
Cent (1859–1970)	68,230.211	400.063	0.59%
2 cent	45.6	9.022	19.79%
3 cent (nickel)	31.378	2.145	6.84%
3 cent (silver)	42.736	21.805	51.02%
5 cent	11.355	257.725	2.27%
½ dime	97.6	1.322	1.355%
10 cent	10,055.455	386.762	3.85%
20 cent	1.355	0.410	30.27%
25 cent	4,449.108	312.175	7.02%
50 cent	1,799.917	176.047	9.78%
$1 (silver)	855.661	331.632	38.76%
$1 (trade)	35.965	1.721	4.79%
$1 (gold)	19,874	0.029	0.15%
$2.50 (gold)	20.426	3.101	15.185
$3 (gold)	.539	.008	1.51%
$5 (gold)	70.911	26.103	33.08%
$10 (gold)	57.683	26.993	46.8%
$20 (gold)	174.105	67.798	38.984%

Note: Figures in millions and rounded. Source: Annual Reports of the Director of the Mint for the years 1867 to 1970.

This odd $3 denomination was struck from 1854 to 1889. The denomination was never particularly popular. In its first year, 138,618 coins were struck. By 1879, it had dwindled to 3,000 circulation strikes and 30 proofs.

A $2.50 gold piece weighing about a quarter of an ounce of gold, actually 0.241875 troy ounces. They were struck until 1929.

The double eagle or $20 gold piece was produced for circulation from 1850 to 1933. It contains 0.9675 troy ounces of gold (33.4 grams of .900 fine gold). About one third of all gold $20 gold pieces made were eventually melted.

Thus, almost four out of every ten double eagle $20 gold pieces minted wound up melted and destroyed. Nearly half of all $10 gold pieces, a solid third of all $5 gold pieces, about 38 percent of all silver dollars, and slightly more than half of all trimes (the silver three cent piece) were melted by the Mint.

Regardless, the collector cannot rely on quantities minted, alone. There was also substantial private melting of coins in the 1960s, when silver prices skyrocketed; in the 1970s; in 2006, when the Mint moved to legally ban the melting of cents because of the high price of copper; and at other times. Because virtually all of this is unrecorded, government minting records are at best only a starting point.

Quantities in Circulation

The next part of determining rarity and value has to do with how many coins actually entered circulation, and how many remain there to be discovered. In some cases, the government has retained a supply of coins in its own vaults—often unknowingly—only to release them to the public. The 1903-O silver dollar—a rarity in the 1950s but common after 1963—is an example.

In the 1950s, coin collecting began to grow as an industry. The notion that the market for collectors was growing was not lost on those involved in the field: In 1952, *Numismatic News* began publication as a biweekly and in 1960, *Coin World* commenced publication as a weekly periodical; *Numismatic News* followed suit before mid-decade. *The Coin Dealer Newsletter*, a pricing guide, began on a weekly basis in 1963, and a teletype service to quote prices was utilized within the industry.

While this was taking place, the price of silver

LEFT: The trime or 3 cent piece was made from 1851 to 1873; there was a move during World War II to revive the denomination, which is a mere 14 mm in diameter, and call it a "paddy." RIGHT: The 3 cent (nickel) was produced from 1865 to 1889 and is in fact copper-nickel. Its 17.9 mm diameter is larger than the silver trime. Its modest mintages suggest a lack of success in the court of public opinion.

increased, an event that would not only affect the coin industry, but shake the American economy. It began innocently enough in 1961 when the price of silver went from $0.91 an ounce up to $1.04. By the next year, it had reached a high of $1.22, and in 1963, the price hit $1.29, the level at which melting silver coins became theoretically worthwhile. The silver price of $1.29 an ounce remained steady for the next four years, which precipitated broad interest in coins—since, in light of the experience with gold, they seemed likely to increase substantially in value.

As of 1963, the Treasury Department still honored the contractual language contained in silver certificates (dollar bills redeemable for silver), and redeemed each certificate for a single silver dollar. Hoards of silver certificates were redeemed, causing a virtual run on the Treasury. In the process, bags of previously rare silver dollars—many dated 1903 from the New Orleans Mint—were discovered. Virtually overnight, pieces which had been scarce plummeted in price from $1,500 per coin to $30 per coin. (The mintage figure—4.45 million pieces—never changed. What did change was quantity in circulation.)

The run on silver also brought the government into the coin business as a full-fledged partner, since in the course of housecleaning and dealing with silver a hoard of 2.9 million rare Carson City minted silver dollars was found in the Treasury vaults. That hoard, eventually sold by the General Services Administration (GSA) for tens of millions of dollars, was the government's first experience with selling coins as an investment; it formed a

This 1903-O silver dollar was once a great rarity . . . and then the Treasury Department opened its vaults. Overnight, the price dropped from $1,500 a coin (in 1963) to $30 a coin (1964).

basis for commemorative coin sales programs and marketing efforts of the Mint in later years that proved durable and successful, raised hundreds of millions of dollars, and assisted in popularizing coin collecting and coin investing. The GSA sold tens of thousands of some dates, and hundreds of thousands of others, in what amounted to a lottery auction sale. The sale destroyed the market value for otherwise rare coins; it took more than a generation for the "CC" mint-marked silver dollars to recover, though once absorbed into the marketplace the value began to come back.

There are dozens of specialty books and many articles designed to help collectors learn about what is rare or scarce, and pricing guides to assist in evaluating the worth of a find or just a particular coin. There are also a number of online pricing guides that can be of assistance. The online library of the American Numismatic Society and The American Numismatic Association is a ready source of information.

Condition

The overall condition of a coin has a significant impact on its price. Generally, identically dated coins will be priced the same if their condition is identical. If one is in poor condition, another in very good condition, and another in about uncirculated, generally the better-conditioned coin will be worth more and sell for more.

Provenance

Provenance, or pedigree, is an often misunderstood factor in the process of evaluating coins. The collection that a coin is from can be important. For example, Congressman Jimmy Hayes was known to have a discerning eye for proof and high quality uncirculated coins, so most coins from his collection are desirable. While coins from the famous collection of King Farouk of Egypt might seem enticing, Farouk hurt their value by cleaning his coins, something a serious collector would not do.

The real importance of pedigree lies less in the individual ownership of a particular coin than in the history of the sale of the coin. The way a coin increases in value over time shows how the market moves as a whole. For example, the 1973 sale of the Reed Hawn Collection of United States Coins sold an 1866 motto, brilliant uncirculated gem half dollar for $475 as lot 232. The purchaser was a man who later became a U.S. Congressman representing a district in Louisiana. The collection was sold again in 1985, and the coin opened at $3,000

1866 motto half dollar. The "no motto" in proof is unique. Half dollars were never a widely circulated coin, perhaps because of their bulkiness.

and sold for $5,775. In the span of a dozen years, the coin had increased in value more than tenfold.

Of course, not every coin with a seemingly impressive pedigree goes up in value. For example, the Robison Collection of United States Coins included a George Clinton cent (of New York State) struck in 1787. Its pedigree showed that it was originally sold in the November 12, 1974 sale by Stack's for $21,000. In the Bicentennial year, the May 26, 1976 sale by Stack's recorded a $23,000 price for the coin; the 1982 price was $14,000.

Here's a listing of prices over time that the 1794 silver dollar has realized:

This NGC MS-61 1794 silver dollar sold for $747,500 in a 2005 Long Beach sale by Heritage. The year 1794 is the first that silver dollars were made at the Mint in Philadelphia. Fewer than 2,000 pieces were produced.

1794 Silver Dollar
Selected Sales in Uncirculated

Sale date		Price Realized
1903	Murdoch collection	$230
1912	Earle collection (Chapman)	$620
1945	World's Greatest (FCC Boyd)	$2,000
1946	Atwater (Mehl) lot 185	$1,575
1947	Mehl (Will Neil)	$1,250
1949	ANA Convention (Numismatic Gallery: Kosoff-Kriesberg) x-Boyd	$1,800
1950	Stack's Fixed Price List # 47, 1950, to B.M. Eubanks x-Boyd	$1,595
1956	ANA Convention (J. Kelly)	$8,000
1957	Stack's Empire Collection (x-Atwater)	$6,500
1958	ANA Convention (Kosoff)	$7,750
1967	Christie's (Lord St. Oswald)	$11,500
1973	Quality (x-Eubanks, Boyd)	$51,000
1973	Superior (to Ralph Andrews)	$110,000
1974	Gibson Groves sale (Stack's)(x-Atwater) x-Empire	$32,500
1975	Bowers & Merena Newport Collection x-St. Oswald	$75,000
1983	Heritage (Steve Ivy) Charlmont Collection x-Eubanks, Boyd	$121,000
1984	Stack's (Carter) x-Neil (Specimen-66, PCGS)	$264,000
1985	Stack's (Hayes) (PCGS-66)	$220,000
1986	Superior (Carmichael) x-Carter, Neil	$209,000
1988	Bowers & Merena (Norweb) (PCGS MS-63) x-St.Oswald	$242,000
1992	Bowers & Merena (Somerset) (x-Eubanks, Boyd) lot 1300	$115,500
1995	Stack's (Numisma '95) (x-Boyd)	$577,500
1999	Bowers & Merena (Bass) (NGC, MS-62)(x-Atwater)	$241,500
2005	Am. Numismatic Rarities Cardinal (x-Boyd)(MS-64, NGC) Green-Boyd-Leland Rogers	$1,150,000
2005	MS61 x-Bass x Murdoch (1903)	$747,500

1794 Dollar: An American Classic

The 1794 silver dollar is an American classic. Authorized by the Mint Act of April 2, 1792, it took almost two years before the Mint director and coiner were properly bonded and metal was obtained to strike the first American silver dollar.

David Rittenhouse, the first director of the United States Mint, deposited silver bullion to be used to manufacture the coins. The bullion varied greatly as there were many gas bubbles in the silver ingots. These imperfections caused laminations and planchet cracks in the coins. Problems such as these plagued approximately 30 percent of the 1794 dollar population.

The 1794 silver dollar was first manufactured on October 15, 1794. All of the coins produced on that day were delivered to Rittenhouse who passed them out to friends. Some were kept as souvenirs while others were spent and circulated. Only 1,758 pieces were minted, and perhaps as few as 140 pieces are known today.

In October 1973, Larry Goldberg, then of Superior Galleries, called the newsroom of *Numismatic News Weekly*, in Iola, Wisconsin, to announce with pride and some measure of awe, "We just sold the world's first $100,000 coin."

That coin that set the record? An uncirculated 1794 silver dollar, which television producer Ralph Andrews acquired for his collection.

Mintmarks

Mintmarks on United States coinage, though similar in purpose to control marks that appeared on the coins of ancient Greece and Rome, originated officially in the year 1838, when the first branch mint was opened at New Orleans and an "O" was utilized to distinguish the coins struck there from those struck at other mints. Mintmarks have had a permanent place on United States coinage ever since. Through the years, various initials have been used to designate minting facilities, as follows:

C: Charlotte, North Carolina (gold coins only), 1838 to 1861

CC: Carson City, Nevada, 1870 to 1893

D: Dahlonega, Georgia (gold coins only), 1838 to 1861

D: Denver, 1906 to present

O: New Orleans, 1838 to 1861; 1881 to 1909

P: Philadelphia, 1792 to present

S: San Francisco, 1854 to 1955; 1968 to present

W: West Point, 1984 to present

Collectors find mintmarks significant, as can be seen in the case of the 1838 half-dollar. Some 3,546,000 of these pieces were produced at the Philadelphia mint, and a mere 20 were struck at the New Orleans mint. In 1984, a coin company sold an 1838-O half-dollar as a proof for $55,000; in 2005, Heritage sold one at auction for

$632,500. By contrast, uncirculated 1838 half-dollars fetch only a few hundred dollars in numerous auction sales.

Grading

Grading is an attempt to quantify and describe the state of preservation and relative condition of a coin. It is an examination of the surface of the metal, the strength of the strike, the luster or sheen that time has given the piece, and its eye appeal. Most professionals acknowledge that when they assign a grade to a coin, they are also assigning a price to it: what they would pay for a particular coin, or what they would sell it for.

In a market that is not homogeneous, the prices differ; so do the various described grades. Lack of a single definitive standard has a great deal to do with the comparative nature of grading.

This 1838-O half dollar, an NGC branch mint proof-64, sold for $632,500 at a 2005 Heritage sale. The use of mintmarks did not begin until 1838, and continues to this day at "D" Denver, "S" San Francisco, "W" West Point and "P" Philadelphia. New Orleans "O" ceased operations in 1909.

Grading coins is not unlike comparing great wines, where adjectives, or even numbers alone, cannot adequately convey a subjective impression, though many try to use various systems to do so. Just as Robert Parker may rate a wine 100 and the *Wine Spectator* may grade the same wine a 95, both are right, to their own standards. If "the best" example known to a grader, cataloguer, or collector changes over time, so inevitably does the point of comparison.

Coin grading may also change perceptibly with time. For example, in 1963, dealer Abe Kosoff—who later pioneered the American Numismatic Association's efforts in the grading field—catalogued the Lahrman Collection, which he offered for sale at auction. Lot 163 was a large cent minted in 1793, Sheldon Variety 11a. Kosoff had earlier catalogued and sold the same coin in 1944 as part of the Oscar Pearl Collection, where he graded it Fine-12. In 1963, he redefined his earlier opinion and now termed it Fine-15—a better grade—and it brought a higher price than estimated, indicating that the buyer agreed with the assessment. There are also numerous examples of coins that are identically graded and sold at widely disparate prices at the same public auction—evidence that at least some buyers believed that the coins were in different condition than the professional cataloguers described.

In a world of subjectivity, where each element is inherently non-objective, it is nonetheless important to collectors and coin buyers to have a fundamental basis under which comparative evaluation can take place. Over the decades, dozens of articles and a

1793 large cent fine-15. Large cents were the first to be graded on the 1 to 70 Sheldon scale. Fine 15 is not as good as it sounds.

However, unlike the adjectives, which referred to wear, Dr. Sheldon's methodology was designed to refer to *price*. For example, a coin in fine-12 condition was to be equivalent to one-fifth the price of an uncirculated-60 coin, even though the wear on the coin is nowhere nearly as substantial as the numbers might suggest. Under this scenario, MS-65 is valued at about 10 percent more than MS-60.

To briefly summarize, coins may generally be termed poor, good, very good, fine, very fine, extremely fine, about uncirculated, or uncirculated, or as a proof or specimen coin intended for collectors. Poor is the low end of the scale; uncirculated is the high end. Generally, the higher the grade, the greater the value for the same coin, and the more desirable to collectors. Although there were a number of adjectives that could be utilized to describe coins, the 1956 *Guide Book of United*

number of books have attempted to do this with respect to the grading of numismatic items.

What seems certain is this common denominator: Grading or describing the condition of a coin continues to be what it always has been—a highly subjective interpretive opinion. Nonetheless, there are certain parameters or limits that can be drawn.

Coin grading standards were quite limited even as recently as a half-century ago. Descriptions were used in a very general way by collectors and dealers alike, and meant different things to each buyer and seller.

Numerical grading shifted with the 1948 publication by Dr. William Sheldon of *Penny Whimsy* (also known as *Early American Cents 1793–1814*), a book that attempted to quantify grading on large cents. Dr. Sheldon devised a scale based on numbers 1 to 70, which were intended by him to roughly correlate with some of the adjectival descriptions.

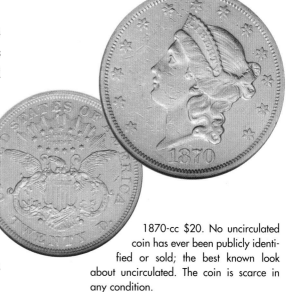

1870-cc $20. No uncirculated coin has ever been publicly identified or sold; the best known look about uncirculated. The coin is scarce in any condition.

Large cents in Good (G-4), Very Fine (VF-35), About uncirculated (AU-58), and better-grade uncirculated (Ms-64) show obvious grading differences.

States Coins (10th Ed.) is typical of grading practices during that gestational period of time in the coin market: For most items, coins were priced in good, fine, and uncirculated condition. Where examples were known, proof was also listed.

To understand these three conditions of good, fine, and uncirculated, create a mental image of a twelve-inch ruler, with the numbers running left to right. Generically, "good" is at the left end, perhaps at the one-inch mark, referring to a well-worn coin, of the type that had been in pocket change for a substantial period of time. The "fine" coin is in the middle, perhaps at the six-inch mark; its design elements are all quite clear, but it, too, has been in circulation.

A typical uncirculated coin is a "10," with all

Proofs

Proof coins have been struck by the United States Mint almost from its founding, and Breen's seminal *Encyclopedia of United States and Colonial Proof Coins* shows examples going back to the copper disme of 1792.

The manufacture of unquestionable proofs appears to have begun on a consistent basis in 1817, according to Breen, but not until 1834 were proof sets produced—and then they were used for purposes of diplomacy. The King of Siam proof set, containing the 1804 silver dollar, is one example of this.

In 1858, Mint director James R. Snowden began to advertise the availability of individual proof coins and proof sets. Early sets were offered by the Mint to customers who frequently ordered by mail. For some customers, such as T. Harrison Garrett, the Mint sent extended explanations. In 1880, Garrison transmitted two drafts totaling $51 to the Mint of the United States at Philadelphia. On February 10, 1880, Superintendent A. Loudon Snowden wrote that the Mint was sending by Adams Express a gold proof set of 1880 (cost, $43) and two silver sets (cost, $4 each). In the same letter, which Bowers published in his extensive book on the collection, Snowden revealed that the gold proof sets "were delivered to us just one hour ago."

The 1880 silver set (actually minor coins and silver) that Garrett purchased were sold by Bowers & Ruddy in October, 1980 during the dispersal of the fabulous collection that later reposed at Johns Hopkins University.

1895

Ed Frossard, a well-known auctioneer a century ago, conducted his 133rd sale on June 14, 1895. A highlight included an 1856 flying eagle cent, one of about 2,000 pieces struck, for which an uncirculated specimen brought $4.45. A U.S. large cent from 1804, broken die, in good condition, yielded five dollars.

That year, the rarest coin in the British Museum collection was a 5 shilling piece of the old pretender issued under James III, only one known. It belonged to General Yorke-Moore, who took it to the Crimea as a talisman. The coin was purchased after the general's death for £250, the largest sum expended by the British Museum for a single coin to that time.

According to *The Numismatist*, the rarest coin in the world, now in the Bibliotheque Nationale Paris, is a gold coin of Eucratides, King of Bactria, about three inches in diameter, which was sold for £1,300 to the French emperor.

that number connotes. The piece is not actually "uncirculated," for if it had somehow never entered circulation, it would not have left the mint. Rather, it never entered into general circulation for a protracted period of time. It still has its mint sheen, is bright, shiny, and with few contact (or "bag") marks on its surface. Imagine it to be similar to a brand-new copper penny fresh from the bank. All other grades can be found along the continuum of the ruler.

From 10 to 12 on the ruler are "better" grades of uncirculated. Forty years ago, dealers and collectors distinguished between a typical uncirculated coin, and one that was better preserved or had fewer blemishes. In catalogues and guidebooks of three decades ago, it is not uncommon

to see various series or designs graded differently, or even priced in fewer than three or four conditions, something that is unlikely today.

In 1958, Brown & Dunn's *A Guide to the Grading of United States Coins* (commonly called *Brown & Dunn*) revolutionized the coin field. It systematically described circulated coins for the first time, in a comprehensive way. There have been many other articles and books written about grading coins before and since, but each owes *Brown & Dunn* a debt of gratitude, for the illustrations of coin wear on a wholesale basis, albeit with line drawings, forever changed the way that coins were described: a verbal description was enhanced to an image.

Photograde was authored by James F. Ruddy in 1970, and was the logical extension of *Brown & Dunn*. According to Ruddy, the book was created because of a "paradox of excellent progress in pricing information but very little that is new in grading guidelines since 1958." That guide modernized the field, marking the first commercial attempt to systematically photograph each type of coin in all of its varying circulating grades. It also demonstrated that photographs could show the differences in various states of grading preservation. *Photograde* depicts coins in about good, good, very good, fine, very fine, extremely fine, and about uncirculated conditions. "Since an uncirculated coin should have no wear it would be difficult to show the absence of wear in a photograph."

Most experienced collectors, and dealers, can differentiate between a typical uncirculated coin (MS-60) and a choice uncirculated (MS-63) spec-

The nickel is a workhorse in the economy. Here are a shield nickel (struck 1866 to 1883), a Liberty nickel (1883–1913), Buffalo (1913–1937), and Jefferson design (since 1938). Only the Jefferson has had multiple reverses of substance.

imen. Most can also distinguish between a technically graded MS-65 and an MS-63 coin. There are those who believe they can identify, time after time, without error, intermediate grades such as MS-61, MS-62, and MS-64 (without confusing an MS-64 with an MS-63 or MS-65, for example).

This is unlikely, however, for even the best of the graders will frequently admit that they may view a point differently in the morning than they will at the end of a tired day, and that the perception of whether or not a coin is MS-63 or MS-64 (representing a significant price difference in the marketplace) will often depend on demand, meaning that grading is market-driven. Purely anecdotal research suggests that when aided by a computer, a competent grader can correctly assign the same grade as the computer about seven times in ten.

A coin's grade is also a shorthand way of describing the coin's condition. Along with the rarity and demand for the coin, its grade is an important basis for establishing a buying and selling price. Unlike other *objet d'art*, a coin cannot be repaired or added to without detracting from its grade. Its condition can worsen with time. A coin cannot improve its condition; however, there are many examples where coins submitted to grading services have improved on subsequent submissions. There are also instances where coins have had grading descriptions dramatically lowered. Even experts have difficulty consistently identifying condition. In grading, there are few absolutes.

There are a number of commercial grading services that will offer a collector or dealer an opinion as to a coin's grade, which in turn allows

The 2 cent piece circulated from 1864 to 1873. It is still a legal tender, but is today worth far more than face value. This is the first coin to bear the "In God We Trust" motto.

the use of a pricing guide to determine a coin's worth. The services do not often agree with each other, especially on crucial differences such as whether a coin is MS-63, MS-64, or MS-65. In one famous case that was brought in the United States Tax Court, two leading grading services were used to grade coins worth millions of dollars. As the court itself relayed the result: over 180 coins were submitted to Professional Coin Grading Service (PCGS) for grading. The conclusion: sixty-nine were proof-63, seventy-eight were proof-64 and twelve were proof-65. There was just one found to be proof-66, one proof-67, and one proof-69.

The coins were then shipped to Numismatic Guaranty Corporation (NCG), whose experts had a different view of part of the collection. They agreed that there was one proof-69, but after that they parted company. NGC's findings: there were five proof-67s, twenty-two that graded proof-66, fifty-one that graded proof-65, seventy-one that graded proof-64, and only twenty-one that graded proof-63. In contrast to the fifteen pieces PCGS found to be 65 or better, NGC ruled seventy-eight to be in that state of preservation.

A non-exclusive list of some of the better known commercial coin grading concerns appears below.

There are books, newspapers, newsletters, and

Silver half dimes (face value 5¢), were manufactured by the Mint from 1794 until 1873. Two types are shown here: bust (for the exposed bosom) and Liberty seated.

The quarter is an economic dynamo; it stays in continuous circulation. First struck in 1796, the examples shown here are bust type; Liberty seated; the Barber design, and standing Liberty.

online resources to use to find out what individual items are worth. A serious collector will subscribe to a periodical or service that provides a ready answer to that question. In the final analysis, the worth of a coin is what a willing buyer and willing seller agree to, or whatever price it brings on the open market.

Acronym	Name	Website	Location
ACCGS	American Coin Club Grading Service	www.accgs.org	Beverly Hills, CA
ANACS	Certification Service, Inc.	www.anacs.com	Austin, TX
HCGS	Hallmark Coin Grading Services	www.hcgshallmark.com	Vancouver, BC, Canada
ICG	Independent Coin Grading Company	www.icgcoin.com	Englewood, CO
NGC	Numismatic Guaranty Corporation	www.ngccoin.com	Sarasota, FL
NTC	Numistrust Corporation	www.numistrust.com	Boca Raton, FL
PCGS	Professional Coin Grading Service	www.pcgs.com	Newport Beach, CA
PCI	PCI Inc.	www.pcicoins.com	Rossville, GA
SEGS	Sovereign Entities Grading Service	www.segscoins.com	Chattanooga, TN
SGS	Star Grading Services	www.stargrading.org	Bellville, OH

CHAPTER EIGHT

IS IT GENUINE?

Coin collecting is a lot more fun today than it was two generations ago, when the counterfeiting of ancient and modern coinage was out of control. Throughout history, criminals have produced coins and paper money that aimed at taking the profit between the value of the metal in the coin and its face value, or, by debasing the metal, making a greater profit. By contrast, the counterfeiters of the latter part of the twentieth century were devoted to taking the numismatic profit, robbing collectors in the process.

There are several different types of numismatic counterfeits that differ from the legal definition, which definition refers to currently circulating legal tender coins. If a tetradrachm of Greece is cast or struck today so that it is indistinguishable from an original, then sold to an American collector, the government of Greece or of the United States cannot arrest the perpetrator for counterfeiting, because the coins of the ancients are neither contemporary nor legal tender. Nonetheless, serious collectors would call such a coin counterfeit.

Another type of counterfeit is where an original, genuine mint product has something added to it, changing its appearance and/or value. An 1889 silver dollar, for example, is worth under $200 in uncirculated condition (MS-65). An identical coin with the two mintmark

OPPOSITE: $20 Liberty gold coin.

Greek (Ionia) tetradrachm circa 160 B.C, has a 32 mm diameter. Greek portraiture and design was unequaled in the ancient world. Even today, some modern coins emulate the style of the Greeks.

1889-cc silver dollar, made at the Carson City Mint. The government sold a small quantity of these coins in the 1970s after finding them in the Treasury Department vaults in Washington.

initials ("CC") beneath the eagle's tailfeather on the reverse is worth hundreds of thousands of dollars in the same condition. It didn't take long for malefactors to see the possibility of making a profit by adding a little metal to a coin.

Some of the techniques utilized to achieve this are downright astonishing. A 1909 cent with the initials "VDB" on the reverse—for designer Victor

David Brenner—is worth about twenty dollars in uncirculated (MS-63) condition; about twenty-eight million pieces were minted at the Philadelphia Mint (using no mintmark) before public outcry over the initials resulted in the mint pulling the coin design and switching to one without the VDB, seventy-two million of which were produced.

Anti-counterfeiting Exhibit

Counterfeit paper money was the focus of a permanent exhibit put together in 2002 by the United States Secret Service for the House Financial Services Committee. Included in the Secret Service's display are examples of counterfeit U.S. currency seized by the Secret Service around the globe.

During fiscal year 2001, approximately $47.5 million in counterfeit U.S. currency was successfully passed, approximately $12.6 million was seized, and over 5,200 arrests were made. Overall, according to Treasury Department statistics, $751.5 billion worth of Federal Reserve notes and $263 million in United States notes remain outstanding; of this, about $611.7 billion remains in circulation.

By contrast, about 3.4 billion dollar coins, and about $29 billion worth of subsidiary and minor coinage, are in the circulation pool. Of the out-standing currency in circulation, more than $421 billion consists of $100 bills—many of which circulate abroad. The next highest denomination is $100 billion worth of $20 bills.

Thus, an infinitesimally small portion (.00000006%) of the American currency system was compromised with counterfeit notes—an amazing record given that American paper currency circulates the world over.

The House Financial Services Committee states that less than .02 percent of the currency in U.S. circulation is counterfeit. Approximately 40 percent of the counterfeit money seized and passed within the U.S. was produced in Colombia. During fiscal year 2001, authorities from the U.S. and Colombia arrested sixty-five suspects, shut down sixteen manufacturing plants, and seized over $78 million in counterfeit U.S. currency.

The mint in San Francisco, using the "S" mint-mark, and "VDB" on reverse, struck 484,000 before they, too, were changed; 1,825,000 of the changed version were struck.

In the 1960s, a technique was invented to drill out the rim of a genuine 1909 VDB cent, anneal it (heat it up to near the melting point of copper), insert a metal "S" into the drilled-out area, and push it through to the surface. Behold: a "perfect" 1909 VDB cent—and a change in value of over a thousand dollars.

There are a number of well-known examples of coins that are numismatic counterfeits. A number of 1944-D cents were ground down to try and create a 1914-D cent. A known non-numismatic counterfeit is the 1944 nickel without the "P" mintmark over the dome of Monticello. (From 1942–1945, the Mint put large mintmarks on coins to call attention to the coin's silver content). The coun-terfeiter, making about four cents profit on each coin, forgot that one key detail and was discovered.

If there's one single coin that is often counter-feited, it's the 1804 silver dollar. This coin is widely produced as a cast (not struck) copy throughout Asia. Vietnam-era veterans found them in Thai-land, and today examples abound throughout southeast Asia. Generally, the counterfeit comes with a story—a tall tale—but the result is that the buyer is usually left fifty dollars poorer.

Gold Coins

Gold coins have been widely counterfeited in the modern era for numismatic purposes.

After private gold ownership was outlawed by the Roosevelt Administration, only rare and unusual coins were permitted to be held by Ameri-cans. Eventually, an entire government bureaucracy, the Office of Domestic Gold and Silver Operation (ODGSO), was set up to govern pri-vate gold ownership. This office set up its own standards as to

1914-D cent (for mintmark) The 1914-D Lincoln cent is a classic rarity with just 1.1 million minted. The coin is widely counterfeited by adding a mintmark, deleting a line from 1944 dated coins, and other methods. There are not "VDB" initials on genuine 1914-D cent.

$3 gold piece, struck 1854–1889. A total of 539,882 business strikes were produced in a thirty-five-year run, but just 2,058 proof coins. The denomination is scarce and underappreciated.

what constituted rare and unusual—standards which were less than precise. Periodic listings were issued by the ODGSO, but the rationale was unpredictable and inconsistent at best. For example, certain British sovereigns of a relatively common date and mint-mark could be imported because they were produced prior to 1960; yet other highly collectible, substantially more valuable sovereigns were denied entry because they were produced after 1960. Before that, government regulators refused to allow the importation of early proof English gold, highly sought after by many collectors, who paid substantial premiums over the bullion content—which might be described as minimal relative to its numismatic worth.

Never reduced to writing, the ODGSO rationale, inconsistency and all, was verbally explained to Harvey G. Stack. Then a prominent dealer, and later president of the Professional Numismatists Guild, he has recounted the rationale publicly on a number of occasions. The Arthur and Ira Friedberg book *Gold Coins of the World* was used as the Treasury guidepost; any coin valued at 25 percent or more above its bullion content in the book, whether in error or appropriately, was deemed "rare and unusual," while anything below

that, even if in obvious error, was denied the requisite import license.

The reason that $20 gold pieces were so frequently counterfeited in the late twentieth century was purely economic. Americans wanted to own gold and were banned by executive order from doing so. A double eagle contains .9675 troy ounces ($33.86 worth of gold at the official price of $35 an ounce that prevailed from 1933 into the 1970s), but the typical uncirculated $20 gold piece routinely sold for $48 in the early 1960s.

Thus, by the simple act of reproducing the coin, a numismatic counterfeiter picked up a profit of 41 percent per coin. That allowed engravers to be hired and expensive minting presses to be safely installed in Lebanon, the Middle East, and Asia to cash in on the profit.

Restrikes

Restrikes are an entirely different numismatic item from counterfeits. Typically, they are produced by government entities themselves for a variety of reasons. In the Massachusetts Bay Colony, the 1652 money was struck bearing that date and design for the next thirty years. In 1741, the Austro-Hungarian

This British sovereign contains 0.2354 troy ounces of gold, or more than $150 worth of gold at today's prices. The sovereign was the coin of choice in the nineteenth century.

When minted, a double eagle had $19.99 cents of gold; after FDR devalued the dollar in 1933, the bullion value of the coin was $33.86. Today, it's over $625.

California Gold Restrike

"There's gold in them thar hills!" was the historic cry that followed the 1848 Sutter's Mill discovery of gold nuggets that marked the start of the California gold rush. What followed was a rich numismatic history as pioneer gold coinage was produced by a series of private mints, all trying to keep up with the trove coming out of the ground.

That event and the days that followed came alive again on August 20, 2001, when restrikes of the historic Kellogg $50 territorial slug were struck on a former San Francisco Mint coining press and counterstamped with a unique, trademarked California Historical Society logo together with the date of striking.

Exactly 144 years before the 2001 striking at the historic Presidio in San Francisco, the gold used for the planchets that produced the restrike had left by boat on the S.S. *Sonora* from San Francisco to Panama.

The cargo manifest contained 330 Kellogg ingots, made by the San Francisco-based gold rush refiner. Each territorial gold ingot weighed between 200 and 500 ounces (worth between approximately $4,000 to $10,000 at the time of casting in 1857).

On arrival at the Isthmus of Panama, the treasure trove was sent by rail to the Atlantic Ocean. It was then stowed on the S.S. *Central America*. The sidewheel steamship *Central America* turned out to be the *Titanic* of her day. Carrying 476 passengers, 102 crew members, and over three tons of precious metal cargo, the ship's hold contained coins from the United States Mint at San Francisco and hallmarked gold bars from Kellogg and four other refiners.

After an uneventful stop in Havana, Cuba, on September 12, 1857, the ship encountered a late summer hurricane and sank about 160 miles off North Carolina, drowning 426 passengers and crew. Its multi-million dollar cargo ended up a mile and a half below the ocean's surface.

In 1988, after years of searching (and 131 years after the ship first sank), the Columbus-America Discovery Group found the *Central America*. After finding the sunken ship, the group brought a proceeding in the U.S. District Court seeking to establish ownership of and the right to salvage the ship and its cargo of gold and other artifacts. Under salvage law, the original owners still retain their ownership interests in such property. It competes with the law of finds which, by contrast, expresses the ancient and honorable principle of "finders, keepers."

Eventually, Dwight Manley, a well-known numismatist and sports agent, acquired all of the gold still held by Columbus-America Discovery Group. Scores of the gold ingots were sold, but about sixty of them were used to produce the planchets for the gold commemoratives whose restrikes recall the fabled gold rush era.

Each commemorative gold piece contains 2.5 ounces of pure gold rush–era gold from large ingots created in 1857 by Kellogg & Humbert, the successor firm to Kellogg & Company. A certificate of authenticity from the California Historical Society accompanies each gold piece.

The first fifty specimens were struck in 2001 on a hydraulic coining press that formerly worked in the San Francisco Mint. Three blows from the coining press were required to bring up the design relief on the massive planchet, the largest ever utilized by mint artist Ron Landis, who oversaw the die transfer process from the original dies.

Empire began producing a trade coin, the Maria Theresa Thaler; today, some 250 years later, the Austrian Mint is still re-striking that coin, and still using a 1780 date. These are non-monetized coins that have bullion value in silver—as the Austrian 100 corona coin has value in gold, the Mexican 50 pesos coin has 1.2 ounces of gold, and many other coins have a similar purpose.

The Massachusetts Bay Pine Tree shillings were deliberately dated 1652 for the succeeding 30 years to allow their production to continue under an old English law.

Collector Coins

Sometimes, the government produces coins to satisfy collector needs. The U.S. Mint, for example, struck several different types of 1804 silver dollars in the 1830s to help the Mint trade for coins they needed for their collections, or simply for outright sale to collectors. None were actually made in 1804, even though Mint records say 19,000 coins were produced. (Historians say the records refer to an earlier period.)

Certification and Protection

Two things simultaneously weakened the scourge of counterfeiting: first, the creation of the American Numismatic Association Authentication Trust (ANAT, later ANACS) certification service; second, passage by Congress of the Hobby Protection Act.

The principal harm that an unauthorized reproduction causes may not stem from the individual who initially creates the reproduction; collectors of ancient coins, for example,

The Mexican 50 peso coin contains 1.2 troy ounces of gold and is a bullion coin not intended for general circulation.

have long made plaster or cement casts of their coins, fired them in kilns, painted them and then studied their intricacies. Some have even used the molds to cast new, modern examples for the purpose of study or photography.

The Hobby Protection Act does not prevent someone from undertaking this type of study; rather, it prohibits the introduction into commerce, by sale or otherwise, of the imitation numismatic item. In 1973, with the passage of the Hobby Protection Act and the regulations promulgated under that law, it became unlawful for anyone to produce an imitation numismatic item unless the word "copy" appears on the item in the statutorily prescribed size and in the appropriate location.

Counterfeit Detection

The United States Secret Service is charged with responsibility for protecting the nation against counterfeits. They maintain a website (www.secretservice.gov) that discusses their core mission. The Secret Service notes that "Genuine coins are struck (stamped out) by special machinery. Most counterfeit coins are made by pouring liquid metal into molds or dies. This procedure often leaves die marks, such as cracks or pimples of metal on the counterfeit coin."

Unlike yesteryear where gold weight was shorted or composition changed from 21.6 karats (.900 fine) to 14 karats (.636 fine), the Secret Service says that "Today counterfeit coins are made primarily to simulate rare coins which are of value to collectors. Sometimes this is done by altering genuine coins to increase their numismatic value. The most common changes are the removal, addition, or alteration of the coin's date or mint marks."

The advice they offer as to how to detect a counterfeit coin is an interesting play on what ANAT/ANACS then said: "If you suspect you are in possession of a counterfeit or altered coin, compare it with a genuine one of the same value."

If you contemplate buying an expensive coin and have doubts about its authenticity, you can always pay a modest fee and submit it to a grading and authentication service. Detection of counterfeit coinage on valuable coins is a job best left to paid experts.

A Trade Secret

One secret worth sharing: most large dealers maintain a file of photos, as well as original counterfeit pieces that they have bought either by mistake or as a courtesy to the marketplace. Counterfeits have diagnostics that are common, and it helps to have a reference point. Comparisons of counterfeits with suspect coins often yield a new counterfeiting technique or a genuine coin. There are few long-time dealers who have not bought "mistakes."

Most serious collectors also have their share. Because selling legal tender counterfeit copies violates the law, and because a good counterfeit is visually similar to an original, it remains hard for any collector to learn specific diagnostic techniques to recognize a counterfeit strike. Suffice it to say that the number of die-struck counterfeit coins is high, but because of commercial grading and authentication companies like PCGS, NGC, ANACS, IGC, and others, and the relatively low cost of examination, losses as a result are now minimal.

Legal Tender

A letter to Alabama's *Huntsville Times* on March 8, 2006 recited how the writer "was recently purchasing gas at Kroger on Hughes Road in Madison when I noticed a sign on the pump notifying customers that 'rolled coins' and 'loose change' could not be accepted as payment. Isn't a business required to accept any form of legal U.S. currency as payment, or can it set its own guidelines for what can be used for payment?"

The answer provided by the newspaper quoted Michael White, spokesman for the U.S. Mint: "There is no law that says a merchant must take any particular kind of currency. Businesses are free to set their own guidelines as to what they accept as payment."

On the Treasury Department's website, the question is asked in a different way, but with the same answers. The Treasury says "The pertinent portion of law that applies to your question is the Coinage Act of 1965, specifically Section 31 *U.S.C.* § 5103, entitled 'Legal tender,' which states: 'United States coins and currency (including Federal reserve notes and circulating notes of Federal reserve banks and national banks) are legal tender for all debts, public charges, taxes, and dues.' "

They go on to explain that "This statute means that all United States money as identified above are a valid and legal offer of payment for debts when tendered to a creditor. There is, however, no Federal statute mandating that a private business, a person, or an organization must accept currency or coins as payment for goods and/or services."

Summarizing its position, Treasury goes on to say that "Private businesses are free to develop their own policies on whether or not to accept cash unless there is a State law which says otherwise. For example, a bus line may prohibit payment of fares in pennies or dollar bills. In addition, movie theaters, convenience stores, and gas stations may refuse to accept large denomination currency (usually notes above $20) as a matter of policy."

CHAPTER NINE

MANAGING YOUR COLLECTION

The difficult decisions many people have once they start to collect are: how to display and store their collection; how to make and maintain a record of their holdings; how to care for their coins; when to upgrade or prune a holding; and finally how to dispose of a collection.

Displaying and Storing Your Collection

Once a collector begins to acquire coins, a decision must be made as to how to protect them— that is, do you retain them in inexpensive coin sleeves, put them in higher quality plastic holders, encase them in the safety of a sealed container, put them in an album, or find another method acceptable to your collecting mode.

A typical coin container is a polyethylene holder that covers the face and the reverse of the coin like a contact lens with wide rims, forming a seal that keeps out dirt, and minimizes the danger of exposure. Coins can also be encapsulated, within 2 inch by 2 inch holders by companies such as Professional Coin Grading Service (PCGS) or NGC (Numismatic Guaranty Corp.). Grading organizations such as these will guarantee the grade or condition of the coin at

OPPOSITE: 1856 Flying Eagle cent.

Encapsulated coins

The Professional Coin Grading Service (PCGS) was founded in February 1986 and was the first company to both encapsulate and grade coins. A few decades later, PCGS certified its 11 millionth coin on May 26, 2005. The milestone coin was a 1990 American Eagle gold $50 graded PCGS MS 69.

PCGS cases are rectangular shaped plastic holders molded to tightly fit a coin and hold the coin safe from the elements or mishandling. The holder is sealed and tamper-proof, with the grade and special characteristics added to the label.

The PCGS has certified several of the world's most valuable rare coins, including: the unique 1794 Flowing Hair dollar with a silver plug (PCGS Specimen-66); the Child's specimen 1804 Bust dollar (PCGS PF-67); the famous King of Siam proof set; and the finest known 1913 Liberty Head nickel (PCGS PF-66). PCGS experts authenticated the long-lost Walton specimen 1913 Liberty Head nickel after the family re-discovered it in 2003.

the time of encapsulation. Once they are encapsulated the coins are kept safe from further wear and exposure to harmful substances.

Another option is to place your coins into inexpensive albums made of cardboard. Several manufacturers have popular albums with acetate slides that cover the coin's surface to prevent damage to the edge, front, or reverse surfaces. Each album may have a specific theme such as state quarters or pennies from a particular time period.

If you decide to display your collection, some prudence is required. Coins and paper money are typically legal tender; they are also small and tempting. They should be displayed in a locked curio cabinet if that is your fancy. Specific collector furniture and coin cabinets, originally built for museum use, can also be a great choice as many have felt-lined drawers which are designed to be lockable while still keeping coinage available for study.

Preparing and Maintaining Inventory Records

It is essential to maintain a current inventory record documenting your coin collection. There are a number of inexpensive computerized programs with templates that can help you do this. The use of a spreadsheet program will also help you organize your holdings and keep track of what you have acquired. At a minimum your inventory list should contain the following information:

Example of encapsulated coin, a Minnesota state quarter "slabbed" by PCGS.

- Date
- Mintmark
- Denomination
- Country of origin
- Condition or grade (also note if the item has been professionally graded, certified or authenticated)
- Size (if unusual or atypical)
- Acquisition cost
- Date of acquisition
- Source (dealer, auction, pocket change, etc.)
- Description
- Serial number
- Catalogue number
- Type number
- Metal
- Inventory number (if applicable)

Additionally you might want to record any special markings, unusual provenance, and "current" value, making sure to note the date of valuation, and updating periodically.

As with all computerized records, be sure to keep a back-up of your data in the form of a hard copy and/or off site electronic copy. Inventory lists can also be kept manually in notebooks but this can quickly become disorganized and unwieldy and is not recommended.

Cleaning coins

If you're thinking about cleaning one or more of your coins, a word of advice: *don't*.

Experts, dealers, intermediate collectors,

Indian head cents were still circulating in worn condition into the 1960s. The author started collecting coins in 1960 as a result of finding a good condition 1906 Indian head cent in pocket change in 1960.

museum curators and metallurgists are unanimous in their view that cleaning a coin strips its surface of metal. This eventually damages the surface sheen and eye appeal—two of the most important aspects that affect grade and price of any numismatic item.

Beginning collectors or novices are often tempted to clean coins by applying jeweler's rouge—a sort of polish—to the surface of a coin.

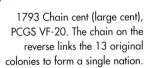

1793 Chain cent (large cent), PCGS VF-20. The chain on the reverse links the 13 original colonies to form a single nation.

That's because molecules of metal have been ripped from the surface of the cleaned portion.

Grading guides refer to the quality of "luster" of the coin and "mint bloom" as important factors in grading coins and in determining their values. Mint bloom is the coloration of a coin as it leaves the coining press. Unattractive luster, such as when the coin is dull, frosty, spotty or discolored, will normally lower the grade of a given coin. Cleaning also damages a coin's luster, decreasing its grade and value.

You can often recognize a cleaned coin by its change in color or altered surface. Copper is notoriously fickle when it comes to cleaning; commercial solvents inevitably yield an unnatural color.

Silver is most responsive to commercial solvents, but repeated use ultimately dulls the surface. For many collectors a cleaned coin calls into question the heritage and provenance of the specimen.

Others will use a commercial liquid tarnish remover for silver, copper, and gold coins. This is a cleaning solution into which coins are "dipped" and, nearly miraculously, they "pop" visually. The coin may look shiny and new but its surface has been irreparably damaged.

To get a sense of how cleaning can damage coins, take a deeply tarnished silver coin that you don't mind damaging and look at it under a magnifying glass. The metal, though dark, should have a pleasing flow and evenness across its surface. Dip a portion (half only) into a metal cleaner and wash off. Under a magnifying glass compare the newly cleaned half with the tarnished half. The tarnished half should have a more even flow than the dipped half.

Design for a proposed coin honoring Ronald Reagan that never advanced once Nancy Reagan opposed replacing FDR on the dime. Reagan was a New Deal democrat who became a Republican later in life and went on to become Governor of California and President. He will be honored on the presidential dollar coin series, probably in 2018.

Among well-circulated but highly collectible coins, dirt and grime may have accumulated in the recesses of the coin; they can be gently removed with a toothpick or cotton swab with the assistance of a liquid such as olive oil or alcohol. An ultrasound bath can also be utilized to shake loose dirt from a coin's surface.

If a coin is improperly stored in a soft plastic holder containing polyvinyl chloride, hydrochloric acid released by the holder can corrode the surface of the coin. In this case the coin must be cleaned in order to prevent further damage. A light acid-dip wash will remove the PVC but this should only be attempted by a professional.

A word is in order about a 21st century phenomenon called "curating" a coin or "coin conservation." The subject is controversial. It involves attempting to restore a coin, that for example, spent years in seawater as buried treasure of a sunken ship, and is meant to give new value to a coin. Curating is a process by which a coin with debris on its surfaces can have that debris removed without harming the integrity of the original surface of the coin. Most collectors prefer a coin that is uncurated to one that is curated.

When to upgrade or prune a holding

In almost every instance, it is better to acquire a coin in superior condition to an inferior example. A collector may choose to acquire a low-graded coin as a placeholder in their collection if a higher-graded one is unavailable or out of financial reach. If the collector is eventually able to obtain a better-graded specimen the recommendation would be to

John Jay Pittman Collection

The extraordinary collection of John Jay Pittman was the result of a lifetime of collecting. Pittman's world-class collection included exceptional examples of early American proof gold coinage, British proof patterns, Japanese coinage, Canadian rarities and a wide range of coins from Mexico and South America.

Significantly, over the past 50 years virtually all of the coins in the collection were placed on display at local coin clubs, regional and state shows, and the ANA national conventions—and many of the holdings were actually written up in The Numismatist, the monthly publication of the American Numismatic Association, as part of the standard show-and-tells from coin club meetings.

What makes the assemblage all the more remarkable is that Pittman, who died the day before his 83rd birthday on February 17, 1996, did not have fabulous wealth. He worked as a salaried employee—a chemical engineer for the Eastman Kodak Company—and bought his coins the way most collectors do, one at a time, over many years.

"prune" the collection and dispose of the lower graded coin.

But that does not mean that a poorly graded coin should not be included in a collection. One example suffices: a large cent graded on the 1 (worst) to 70 (best) Sheldon grading scale, such as a 1793 Sheldon variety Non-collectable-2 (NC-2) in grade basal state-1. A description of the coin shows how awful-looking it is: "a number of minor nicks, digs and scratches consistent with the grade, but only two serious rim dents."

However this particular coin design and variety is unique, and its rarity was recognized by Richard Winsor who acquired it in the immediate post-Civil War period. From there, it passed through the hands of a number of noted collectors and in June 1984, Stack's auctioned this basal-1 cent, at the very lowest end of the grading scale, for mid-five figures.

Lifetime management and planning

The very fact that we keep track of a coin's provenance or pedigree shows how temporary ownership is. Some collectors like Evelyn and Eric P. Newman, solved the problem by setting up their own museum on the campus of Washington University in St. Louis. Others have spectacular auction sales over a period of years to sell off the collections.

For the collector who buys, sells, and acquires a coin collection over a lifetime, it is important to determine what will become of your collection after your passing.

It is best to prepare now because disposition of a collection can be difficult even under the best of circumstances. At such an emotional time it's best to have pre-set instructions that a loved one, or an executor can follow.

The reason for this is clear—your collection has value and to maximize the value of the collection, you may want your heirs to dispose of it in accordance with your wishes, not those of individuals less informed than you.

If you have a strong preference as to a specific way of how you wish your collection to be handled, leave written instructions. For example, you may want to suggest that your coins be sold back to the dealer you acquired them from, auctioned, given to a favorite charity, or that the collection remain intact and be donated to a non-profit museum.

If you decide to leave your collection to an heir, here is a summary of key steps that you can take to facilitate handling of your numismatic estate.

1873 no arrows closed "3" half dollar (reverse), NGC proof-67. The "no arrows" means that this is before the Coinage Law of 1873 went into effect. Arrows at the date signify a weight or law change by Congress.

1796 dime NGC MS-64 The dime was not struck until 1796 (unlike the cent, 1793, and silver dollar, 1794). Robert Scott was the designer of the obverse, John Eckstein the reverse. Only 22,135 were coined, all at Philadelphia Mint, which was still expected to be the temporary site of the Mint until the federal government moved to Washington.

and more importantly also tends to maximize the possibility of receiving the most value for the collection.

If you decide to have the collection auctioned, it is not necessary to have all of it sold by the same auctioneer. Not all auctioneers specialize in the same areas. Some, for example, are more competent in ancient coins than they are in modern foreign issues while other auction houses are excellent with the Old Masters but less than adequate for newer material.

- Be sure that you have a current inventory list of your entire collection and that it is kept updated with accurate values and information. Also make sure that this list is easily accessible.
- Prepare a list of those who you believe might be the best individuals or firms to handle disposition of the collection (can be done by classes of items or individually)
- If you have a friend or colleague who can assist the executor as to pricing, valuation, or disposition, give a name and address.

If you decide to sell your collection, unless you have a long and established relationship with someone in the field, you should require three separate bids. This avoids the possibility of collusion,

Byzantine gold coinage appears crudely designed and struck but is very beautiful. The coinage is similar in design to the mosaics in St. Sophia Church in Istanbul.

CHAPTER TEN

COINS OF DISTINCTION

The story of the founding of the Smithsonian Institution, as well as the story of the Smithsonian National Numismatic Collection, is a story of coinage. The Smithsonian was founded based on the will of James Smithson, and the legacy he awarded to the newly minted United States of America was paid in £1 gold British sovereign coins dated 1838. Two remain in the Smithsonian National Numismatic Collection (also referred to as "the National Coin Collection").

Coins of distinction are found throughout the Smithsonian National Numismatic Collection. Each tells a fascinating story, and each draws "oohs" and "aahs" when it is displayed, either in a Smithsonian exhibit or at a numismatic convention. Important sections of the Smithsonian National Numismatic Collection were acquired by donation from individuals who believed that some major rarities belonged to the nation, rather than to a private collection. What follows are a dozen or so coins of distinction, each with a story to tell, many of which are in the Smithsonian National Numismatic Collection.

Some of these coins, like the 1933 $20 gold piece, have immense value. Others, like the 1864

OPPOSITE: 1933 double eagle (obverse).

2 cent piece, have a mintage in the millions, but a story to tell. Still others, like the 1964 Peace dollar, are lacking in the Smithsonian National Numismatic Collection, but have a strange tale to tell. And then there are the coins like the 1974 aluminum cent whose continued existence was secured by its hurried donation to the Smithsonian.

Errors, circulated coins, uncirculated coins and uncirculated specimens, freshly minted coins, patterns, and trial strikes. Coins of politics, and money of the people. In no particular order, these are their stories.

1933 Double Eagle $20 Gold Piece

The 1933 $20 gold piece has a unique place in collecting history. Designed by famous sculptor Augustus Saint-Gaudens from a design approved by President Theodore Roosevelt, the 1933 $20's celebrated story starts with another Roosevelt—FDR—and the New Deal effort to control the national gold supply as a means of ending the great Depression.

When FDR banned private gold ownership, the 1933 double eagle had been struck at the Mint but not generally released into cir-culation. The Mint melted over 400,000 Saints with a 1933 date and no mintmark (for Philadelphia Mint origin). A few escaped the dustbin of history and the melting heaps, purchased by private collectors for as much as $2,000. The government began seizing them in 1944, and the coins went into hiding. In all, the Mint seized at least nineteen specimens, but a number of coins continued to be traded on the sly, often at relatively high prices. Some well-known collectors even turned them in voluntarily. The beginning of the end came when one example appeared as lot 1681 in the Col. John W. Flanagan sale sold by Stack's on March 25, 1944. The Flanagan coin was seized by the Secret Service, no compensation was offered, and the coin was reputedly melted. At the time of its proposed sale, Stack's claimed in the auction catalogue to know of eight or ten pieces that had been sold privately. They underestimated the number. In 2003 the family of Israel Switt discovered ten 1933 double eagles in a safe deposit box, and sent them to the Mint for authentication. The Mint said they were genuine and declined to return them, claiming that they were stolen government property. In December 2006,

1933 double eagle (reverse). The government sold one at auction for over $7 million a few years ago.

Three years after the only officially recognized specimen brought $7.59 million at public auction, a hoard of ten pieces was seized by the U.S. Mint. The coins have been shipped to Fort Knox, Kentucky, where they are in the secure gold depositary facility along with the remnants of millions of gold coins struck prior to 1933, and then melted after a presidential order by FDR that essentially recalled all but numismatic pieces, then termed "rare and unusual" coins.

1933 $20: One Coin's History

One 1933 double eagle found its way into the collection of Egypt's King Farouk. Farouk's agents located the coin for him in the 1940s, and he made application for it, through diplomatic channels, to be exported from the United States to his palace collection in Egypt. Nellie Taylor Ross, director of the Mint from 1933 to 1953, received the request that it be authorized for export as a "rare and unusual" coin. Egypt was a badly needed ally in North Africa at the time. This appears to be the reason that an export license for the coin was granted.

In 1952, Col. Gamal Abdel Nasser led a *coup d'etat* against Farouk. When Nasser's provisional government seized all of Farouk's assets, including his coin collection, and ordered that they be sold for the benefit of the people of Egypt, the U.S. government formally asked for the double eagle's return. It was withdrawn from the sale, and lost to history for 40 years.

It came back into public life in 1996 where it surfaced in the hands of coin dealer Stephen Fenton and was seized by Secret Service agents. Eventually a settlement was proposed stating that the coin would be sold at auction with the proceeds split between the government and Fenton. In 2002 the U.S. Mint partnered with Sotheby's and Stack's to sell the 1933 double eagle $20 gold piece at public auction in New York City. A fifty-six page catalogue featured the single, unnumbered lot. The public auction for the rare 1933 $20 gold piece—the only one of this type that the government claims a collector can legally own—took place on July 30, 2002, after about six years of protracted litigation.

Everything about the sale was unusual, from the single-lot, large-size catalogue, to the attendance, held in a packed room that could seat upward of 800 people. News camera crews, the daily and international press, as well as dealers and collectors all gathered to see history made by this coin of mystery. The audience responded with a reverence only seen on other historic occasions, such as in 1979 when a Brasher doubloon from the Friedberg Family collection, or an 1804 silver dollar, was offered at the auction block. Bidding moved steadily, if progressively, in $100,000 increments as former Congressman Barry Goldwater, Jr., put in the first bid at over $2 million. About eight live bidders were registered, with several more bidding by telephone. As the sale progressed, and seconds ticked into minutes, there was palpable excitement as the auctioneer hastened the cadence. The entire event took about eighteen minutes and the winning bid, by an anonymous telephone bidder, was $6,600,000—a world's record for a $20 gold piece or any other coin.

Where an ordinary bill of sale accompanies most auctions, this one also had a unique engraved bill of sale and transfer of title prepared for the United States Mint and engraved by the U.S. Bureau of Engraving and Printing—signed by the Director of the U.S. Mint Henrietta Holsman Fore, and Associate Director of Sales, David Pickens.

Swift's descendants brought suit to regain possession in a federal court case that is expected to last for years.

The Mint stores its ten coins in Fort Knox, but has periodically removed them for an impressive public display using armed guards, most recently at the annual convention of the American Numismatic Association, held in Milwaukee in August 2007. The 1933 double eagle remains a coin of distinction, as well as one of mystery.

1913 Liberty Head Nickel

Only five 1913 Liberty head nickels were made at the Mint, probably in the 1920s, but one was destined to become a television star on *Hawaii Five-O*. A perennial evil man played by actor Victor Buono tried to steal what the TV show billed as the world's first $100,000 coin sold in a private treaty sale.

This coin has a long and involved history. In December 1919, a former Mint employee, Samuel Brown, advertised in the American Numismatic Association's monthly periodical *The Numismatist* that he was willing to buy an example of the coin for $500. In 1920, he raised the price to $600.

Evidence today points to the fact that he had actually produced the coins, on Mint machinery, using government dies, on government planchets that awaited the decision of the Treasury chief to change the design to the Indian head and bison reverse.

Eventually, it would come out that there were five specimens produced, all tracing their pedigree to Brown. In the 1920s, they were acquired by Col. Ned Green, and in 1941 came into the possession of Eric P. Newman and Burdette Johnson, in set-tling the Green estate. By late 1941, all five went to Newman, then began to be broadly disbursed.

In the early 1930s, Fort Worth dealer B. Max Mehl organized a national campaign to find the so-called "sixth" 1913 Liberty nickel, offering to pay $50 for it—big money during the Depression—and popu-larizing his mail order business. His advertisement read "Old Money Wanted. Will pay Fifty Dollars for Nickels of 1913 with Liberty head (no Buffalo)." None, of course, were ever turned in—but Mehl reaped publicity in print and on the radio, and went on to become the biggest coin dealer in the world.

The coins changed hands many times over the next few decades, landing in the collec-tions of many prominent dealers and collectors.

In 1972, World Wide Coin Invest-ments of Atlanta bought a specimen from Edwin Hydeman for $100,000—the first time that any coin had reached that price in public auction or private treaty. When the 1913 Liberty nickel was the star of the popular *Hawaii Five-O*, armed guards stood on the set to make sure that the six-figure investment was protected.

The late George Walton's previously lost

ABOVE: 1913 Liberty head nickel, one of five known. Samuel Brown advertised in the ANA's monthly periodical, *The Numismatist*, that he was willing to buy an example of the 1913 Liberty head nickel for $500. In 1920, he raised the price to $600 a coin. Brown was a former Mint employee, and the evidence points to the fact that he had produced the coins, on Mint machinery, using government dies, on government planchets but not on government time.

specimen was rediscovered by his family in 2003 as a result of a publicity campaign engineered by public relations guru Donn Pearlman. He dreamed up the idea of displaying the four known examples of the 1913 Liberty nickel at the World's Fair of Money—otherwise known as the ANA Convention—and undertaking a national awareness campaign to announce that one coin was missing.

And that is why today, the 1913 Liberty nickel remains a coin to be talked about, with a smoke-and-mirrors history.

1974 Aluminum Cent

Aluminum had its day on Capitol Hill on March 27, 1974. This was nearly 170 years after the great British chemist Humphry Davy treated clay sulphuric acid and decided that the clay contained an unknown metal—which he called aluminum.

On that day, the House Subcommittee on Consumer Affairs of the House Banking & Currency Committee heard public testimony on the plan to change the composition of the cent from bronze to aluminum as the answer to the rising price of copper that threatened the seigniorage of the U.S. Mint's most called-for coin.

In the mid-nineteenth century, Henri Deville, a French chemist, discovered the first inexpensive process to break down aluminum chloride into aluminum metal. At the time, gold sold for $20.67 an ounce, or about $250 a troy pound; aluminum was so scarce that its estimated cost, in 1859, was $545 a pound to produce.

Even in 1884, the metal was so rare that the Washington Monument was topped with a 100-ounce aluminum cap, the largest piece of the metal then known in the United States. The novelty of aluminum, besides its light weight, is the ease with which it can be machined—or for a coin, struck.

In 1886 a less expensive production method was discovered. As production levels increased, producers kept the price of aluminum low to encourage its use by manufacturers.

In a 1973 study of alternatives for coining metal, the U.S. Mint examined high feasibility material and rated aluminum "A" and "A+" for ease of coin fabrication and cost, as well as seigniorage protection—the small amount of profit that the government ekes out of each coin produced.

The Mint launched a full-court press upon Congress to authorize an aluminum cent. Mary T. Brooks, mint director, appeared with deputy director Frank H. MacDonald, assistant director for public

Aluminum cent 1974 (obverse). The coins were produced in 1973 with a 1974 date in anticipation of a Congressionally authorized change that never came.

affairs Roy C. Cahoon, and a phalanx of aides. They came with a mounted exhibit of two aluminum cents that were attached to black backboard.

In the time-honored tradition of non-collectors, glue was utilized for the mounting. The hearing was an eye-opener. The Mint was sure it was right, and that aluminum was the answer. Lining up on the other side was the National Automatic Merchandising Association, led by Dick Schreiber, a veteran lobbyist on issues affecting the vending industry.

Schreiber had samples of aluminum blanks that were of the right weight and size, and a rejection mechanism. He used it effectively to demonstrate just how the aluminum cent would jam the "J" curve that is utilized as a rejecter mechanism. (The coin enters at the top of the "J," goes toward the bottom, swings around the curve, and flips upward. If of a proper weight, it goes into the coin box and the transaction is complete; if not, it goes to the rejecter slot. The aluminum coins got stuck). Examples of the aluminum blanks were freely handed out by Schreiber. One of them was presented to the Smithsonian's National Coin Collection.

Other samples of the aluminum cent had evidently been passed among the committee members and staff. Mint records show that at least seven examples went to Texas Representative Wright Patman, chair of the committee, and evidently it was distributed at least to Charles B. Holstein, the staff director of the Consumer Affairs subcommittee.

We know this, retrospectively, because when controversy about the coin arose, Holstein—who had carried the coin as a sort of good luck charm in his wallet for more than six months—promptly took the piece to the Smithsonian, where it resides today, logged into the National Coin Collection.

1964 Peace Dollar

Shades of déjà vu: dealer Bob Cohen ran an advertisement in the April, 1973 issue of *The Numismatist*, offering a reward to anyone leading him to a genuine specimen of the 1964 Peace dollar. Unlike Samuel Brown's offer for a 1913 Liberty nickel, Cohen had not ordered the coin struck and didn't have a specimen.

Origins of the 1964-D silver dollar bearing the Peace design and technical specifications last used in 1935 are mixed up in governmental legerdemain and lost or inaccurate records designed to deliberately deceive those looking into the coin's history.

Historical records show that the President of the United States ordered the production of the coin and that Congress directed that its production be halted.

Much of the story is inferential. An online search of both the LBJ presidential library in Austin, and the Eva B. Adams section of the University of Nevada at Reno yields no clues—though Adams is listed as having called the President on other numismatic matters.

Lyndon B. Johnson, a Texan with a strong Western heritage, was sworn into the presidency following John F. Kennedy's assassination in late November, 1963, just as the budget for the following fiscal year was being framed. At some point, either in the Oval Office or across the street

Copy of the 1964 Peace dollar. No specimens have surfaced on the open market since their production. The same design as the 1921 Peace dollar was utilized when President Johnson directed that it be produced.

in the Main Treasury Building, a decision was made to include an item in both the supplemental appropriation budget for 1964 and for the following fiscal year.

Whether it was Johnson who ordered the inclusion can not be ascertained. In any event, it is clear that he did not object to it. Simply put, the point placed in both budgets was for funds to produce 150 million silver dollars—fifty million from the 1964 supplementary appropriation, and the balance from the regular 1965 submission covering the fiscal year ending June 30, 1966.

The House of Representatives refused to grant any of the requested funding, but the Senate revised the appropriations bill to include $600,000 needed to produce forty-five million silver dollars. The Treasury agreed to the modification, and on August 3, 1964 Johnson signed it as Public Law 88-392.

Manufacture of the coins had to take place during the fiscal year ending June 30, 1965. After that point, new authorization and appropriation would be required; potentially, the same conflict between the House and Senate could result.

On May 15, 1965 Johnson issued a statement indicating that he had ordered production of silver dollars to begin before the appropriation expired on June 30. Trial strikes were made at the Philadelphia Mint immediately following the Presidential directive. The die work had evidently been prepared months before, probably after the appropriation had been authorized. A total of thirty pieces were produced in this first trial striking, and 28 were immediately melted by count. The remaining two pieces were shipped to Washington, D.C., for optical, spectrographic, and physical analysis by the Mint Laboratories. A large production run followed, but was later melted. To this day, no example has ever been displayed in public.

Brasher Doubloon

This is a coin so famous that a movie was named after it. The coin's designer and minter: Ephraim Brasher (pronounced "Brazier"), a New York City goldsmith who, in 1787, lived on Cherry Street beside President George Washington. Only a few examples of the coin are known, including specimens in the Smithsonian national collection. The Smithsonian also has the unique Brasher half-doubloon, dated 1787. Interestingly enough, the correct pronunciation of the designer's name was discovered only recently, when his descendants attended an auction sale of an example of the coin.

In its time, the doubloon had a value of about sixteen Spanish dollars ($15 in colonial New York

No coin is as famous as the Brasher doubloon. Made in New York City, just down the street from President George Washington, they remained out of circulation for many years. The 1921 John Story Jenks sale was termed "recent" until the next public auction in Auction '79 ($435,000).

currency) and may have represented an early attempt to have a national precious metal currency. But no one is quite sure, since so few were struck and no records left behind from the private minter.

The design is ingenious. On the obverse the sun is rising from a range of mountains; in the foreground, the sea. Brasher's name is underneath. The reverse features the ubiquitous eagle with olive branches (symbol of peace) in one talon, arrows (symbol of war) in the other. The "BE" punch is on the eagle's breast.

A century ago, Sylvester Crosby's book *Colonial Coins of America* listed four known coins, and into the early 1970s, the most recent one sold was the fabled John Story Jenks specimen, which Chapman auctioned in 1921 for an astonishing $10,000. In 1979, the specimen owned by the Friedberg family and their firm Coin & Currency Institute was sold by RARCOA as part of Auction '79, and brought

an astonishing $435,000. There have been subsequent sales at increasingly higher prices.

The Brasher doubloon is a mystery coin as to its origin, purpose, and history; its low mintage scarcity has amplified the story and raised its net worth. See an example at the Smithsonian or the American Numismatic Society in New York City; the ANS coin is on loan to an exhibit at the Federal Reserve Bank of New York Museum, 33 Liberty Street, New York City.

1804 Silver Dollar

Here's a coin whose fame starts with the official figures reporting about 19,000 pieces minted. The problem is, those figures were erroneous; in fact, no silver dollars at all were made by the Philadelphia Mint in 1804. In 1834, when the U.S. State Department needed to provide an American proof set to diplomats to present as gifts, the Mint decided it would manufacture silver dollar coins dated 1804, the last year mint records said silver dollars were produced. The reporting error was not discovered until the 1860s.

The design of the coin, made on dies cut in 1834 or 1835, is alluring: a flowing haired Liberty with ample bosom and cleavage; the reverse depicts the eagle of the Great Seal of the United States. Note that the talons contain the ubiquitous arrows and olive branch, between war and peace. The eagle's beak points toward the arrows of war.

One 1804 silver dollar went to the Smithsonian Institution National Coin Collection around 1978, after the decision was made to close the historic holding, begun by Farran Zerbe, that constituted the money museum of Chase Manhattan Bank. There are three known types of this coin; the Smithsonian's is a unique restrike with a plain edge contrasted with the "lettered edge" type that contains different reverse die cuttings. All are novodels, or restrikes, using newly created dies designed to simulate what the coin would have looked like had it been struck in 1804.

The recent 1999 sale of the first reverse "original" 1804 dollar for $4.1 million at public auction was front page news, covered in the *Wall Street Journal* and elsewhere. This has always been the case, even when the Dexter specimen was first auctioned in 1884 for $216.

Legendary 1804 silver dollar (obverse and reverse). "Anna and the King of Siam" is one source for the 1804 silver dollar, which was made in a presentation set sent to Thailand over 150 years ago. All of the dollars were backdated because of a mint bookkeeping error.

Copper cent 1943. If you think you have one, try a magnet first. If it sticks, it's steel with a copper coating.

1943 Copper Cent

The United States was at war, fighting to preserve our national way of life. Congress had already been asked to take copper out of the nickel to help the munitions industry. As the war progressed, it became necessary to remove copper from the cent as well. The War Powers act of 1942 even allowed for a new three cent piece, called a "Paddy," to be struck.

The familiar bronze cent alloy had been unchanged since 1864, but copper was removed and replaced staring in 1943 with a steel cent that was zinc plated to prevent rust.

In 1940, the Mint produced about 800 million cents; the following year, about a billion. In 1943, 1.2 billion steel cents were produced. So were about 24 copper cents with the 1943 date and mintmark. This mint error, probably done with leftover blanks that were put into the hopper and fed unwittingly to the coinage presses, created a major rarity that reminds us, even today, of the trying times of that era.

Other similar coins include 1944 steel cents (also presumably made from erroneously used blanks), and off-metal strikes of blanks intended for foreign coins that the U.S. Mint was contract agent to produce. There's even a 1946 war nickel found in pocket change several years ago, and worth thousands of dollars. The 1944 steel cent has a $10,000 to $12,000 price range based on recent sales; the 1943 copper, multiples of that level.

1838-O Half Dollar

For its first 47 years of existence, the U.S. Mint at Philadelphia had an exclusive franchise in producing American coinage. That changed in 1835 when Congress authorized branch minting facilities at New Orleans, Louisiana; Charlotte, North Carolina; and Dahlonega, Georgia. Of the three southern mints, two were mints of opportunity granted by mini-gold rushes in Northern Georgia and North Carolina. The Mint in New Orleans, on the other hand, was still in operation at the turn of the twentieth century, not closing its doors until 1909.

Located in Vieux Carré, the French Quarter, right on the Mississippi River, the New Orleans Mint was the first of the branch mints to start

Half dollar 1838-O. The first year of issue for a mint-marked half dollar is this rarity. The mintmark is on the obverse.

production, and the first coin produced was an 1838 half dollar. The mint's mark, an "O," appears on the obverse directly above the date.

Whether the first branch mint coins were made in New Orleans or were proof coins struck as a sample in Philadelphia is still the subject of debate. Edouard Brossard, a nineteenth-century dealer and auctioneer, called them die trials made in Philadelphia. Regardless, only about twenty were made, of which about a dozen are known to exist today.

Collectors find mintmarks significant, as can be seen in the case of the 1838 half dollar. Some 3,546,000 of these pieces were produced at the Philadelphia mint, and a mere 20 were struck at the New Orleans mint. In June 2005, Heritage sold one of the finest specimens known for $632,500—a remarkable showing for the first American coin to bear a mintmark. A regular Philadelphia mintmarked coin sells for several hundred dollars.

1864 Two Cent Piece

In the dark days of the Civil War, the future of the United States as a nation was in doubt. The solution of some was to put their faith in Abraham Lincoln, and later in Ulysses S. Grant. Secretary of the Treasury Salmon P. Chase had a different idea: he put the nation's future into faith in the Almighty—in a very public way.

From the records of the Treasury Department, it appears that the first suggestion of the recognition of the deity on the coins of the United States was contained in a letter addressed to the Hon. S. P. Chase, by the Rev. M. R. Watkinson, Minister of

Two cent piece 1864. The motto "In God We Trust" appears atop the shield.

the Gospel, Ridleyville, Pennsylvania, dated November 13, 1861.

"One fact touching our currency has hitherto been seriously overlooked, I mean the recognition of the Almighty God in some form in our coins," Rev. Watkinson wrote.

"You are probably a Christian. What if our Republic were now shattered beyond reconstruction? Would not the antiquaries of succeeding centuries rightly reason from our past that we were a heathen nation? What I propose is that instead of the goddess of liberty we shall have next inside the 13 stars a ring inscribed with the words 'perpetual union'; within this ring the alleging eye, crowned with a halo; beneath this eye the American flag, bearing in its field stars equal to the number of the States united; in the folds of the bars the words 'God, liberty, law.'

"This would make a beautiful coin, to which no possible citizen could object.

This would relieve us from the ignominy of heathenism. This would place us openly under the Divine protection we have personally claimed.

"From my heart I have felt our national shame in disowning God as not the least of our present national disasters. To you first I address a subject that must be agitated."

A week later, on November 20, 1861, Secretary Chase wrote to James Pollock, the Director of the Mint, "No nation can be strong except in the strength of God, or safe except in His defense. The trust of our people in God should be declared on our national coins."

He concluded with a mandate: "You will cause a device to be prepared without unnecessary delay with a motto expressing in the fewest and tersest words possible this national recognition."

In December 1863, the Director of the Mint submitted to the Secretary of the Treasury for approval designs for new one, two and three cent pieces, on which it was proposed that one of the following mottoes should appear: "Our country; our God;" or "God, our Trust."

Secretary Chase replied on December 9, 1863: "I approve your mottoes, only suggesting that on that with the Washington obverse the motto should begin with the word 'Our' so as to read: 'Our God and our country.' And on that with the shield, it should be changed so as to read: 'In God We Trust.'"

The Act of April 22, 1864 created the two cent piece, and Secretary Chase exercised his rights to make sure the motto was in the design.

1838 £1 British Sovereign

The Smithsonian Institution was founded based on a bequest of James Smithson, a British scientist who had never visited the United States. When he was sixty-one years old, Smithson drew a will leaving his entire estate to a nephew, Henry James Hungerford. The will further stipulated that if the nephew died without heirs, the estate would be bequeathed to the United States of America to create and found, at Washington, D.C., an establishment "for the increase and diffusion of knowledge among men."

Smithson died shortly thereafter in 1829. In 1834, Hungerford died without issue. On July 1, 1836, Congress formally accepted the legacy bequeathed to the nation by James Smithson and pledged the faith of the United States to the charitable trust.

Two years of litigation in British courts followed with other putative heirs, led by Richard Rush, a diplomat, recent vice presidential candidate, and son of Dr. Benjamin Rush, a signer of the Declaration of Independence. It took time, but in 1838, British courts approved the bequest. The legacy was 92,635 pounds, 18 shillings and 9 pence. Madame de la Batut, mother of Smithson's nephew, received £5,015, leaving about £87,620 to be converted to currency from the stocks and annuities in which it was held.

Today, the judgment would have been reduced to a bank deposit, and

The coin that helped found a national museum, £1 of 1838.

the funds wired through international banking channels. In 1838, however, it was mostly a cash economy—bills of exchange and paper money simply weren't favored.

Rush's solution was to convert the funds into gold that was a legal tender. He purchased 104,960 new English sovereigns—new, according to Dr. Richard Doty, a modern-day Smithsonian curator, "so there would be no loss of gold through wear." This hoard of sovereigns, bearing the "young portrait" of Queen Victoria (Krause-Mishler number 736.1 variety, Friedberg catalogue number 387) were placed in 105 bags (which cost sixpence apiece), packed 1,000 coins per bag.

Records show that all were shipped, insured, and crossed the Atlantic Ocean on board the *Mediator*, packed into eleven boxes, each weighing 187 pounds. Back in 1837, each of the sovereigns had a weight of .2354 troy ounces of gold, and were worth $4.86 apiece. The coins today in uncirculated condition have a value of more than $700. The Smithsonian has retained two examples of the coin from the original hoard used to create its permanent collection.

The Smithsonian owes its existence to the £1 gold coinage of 1838—since they were used to pay James Smithson's legacy to the United States.

GLOSSARY OF TERMS
USED IN THIS BOOK

Here's a handy glossary of terms to help you converse in coin collecting lingo.

24k 24 karat. Pure 24/24ths. For gold, 22/24ths would be 22k or a fineness of .91666 (typical of British gold coins). American gold coins are generally 21.6k (.900 fine).

.900 fine An alloy of gold mixed with silver and copper or silver mixed with copper in a 90 percent major metal/10 percent nominal metal ratio.

$20.67 The fixed price of gold from 1837 to 1933. By 1837, Congress finally got it right, setting the value of gold at $20.67 an ounce—a rate that would hold for nearly a century and provide substantial stability. Through the California gold field discoveries, the Civil War, the expansion of America, World War I, and beyond, the price held stable.

$42.22 The official price of an ounce of gold in 2007, as it has been for more than 30 years.

Adjustment marks Commonly found on older gold and silver coins, these are evidence of filing down an overweight planchet to bring a coin to legal weight.

American eagles Gold, platinum, or silver coins issued in proof or uncirculated qualities. Gold and platinum coins are issued with one-tenth, one-quarter, one-half, and one ounce precious metal content.

ANA American Numismatic Association, the national coin club, founded in 1891 and chartered by Congress in 1912. Located in Colorado Springs, Colorado.

ANACS Formerly American Numismatic Association Certification and Authentication Service, later Amos Numismatic Authentication & Certification Service. A commercial authentication and grading service which, for a fee, will tell you if your coin is genuine and rate its condition.

Ancient coin A coin made in Rome, Greece, Byzantium, or other countries, generally before A.D. 500.

Annealing The process of heating blanks, in an annealing furnace, to soften them before they are struck into coin.

ANS The American Numismatic Society, founded in 1858, the oldest educational organization of its kind in the U.S. Located in New York City's financial district.

Anthony dollar Susan B. Anthony dollar, authorized by Congress and produced from 1979 to 1981 and again in 1999.

Arrows On a U.S. coin design near the date, symbolizes that a weight change has occurred. When in the talons of the eagle, a symbol of war.

Assay To melt a coin in order to an analyze its weight and metal composition.

Barber coinage Two great engravers at the Philadelphia Mint in the nineteenth and twentieth centuries were father and son, William and Charles Barber. Their coinage designs are universally referred to by their last name, i.e., the Barber dime, Barber quarter and Barber half dollar, all 1892–1916.

Base metals Generally refers to coining metals of copper, nickel, aluminum, zinc, and various alloys or combinations thereof.

Blank A coin before it is struck.

Bronze A copper alloy.

Bullion Generally refers to a precious metal (gold, silver or platinum) in bar or coin form.

Bureau of Engraving & Printing Where the nation's paper money is made, in Fort Worth, Texas and Washington, D.C.

Bust A Roman or Greek style facial portrait facing left or right, common in U.S. presidential coinage portraits. Earlier, a "Bust type dollar" refers to the bosom of Liberty.

Circulating coins Cent, nickel, dime, quarter dollar, half dollar, and one dollar coins used in daily commerce.

Clad coinage Copper/nickel composition in sandwich form authorized by the Coinage Act of 1965, used for dimes, quarters and half dollars.

Coin silver Silver with a fineness of .900.

Coining press The machine that strikes a coin, at speeds upward of 700 coins per minute for the new presidential dollars, to several strikes per minute for proof coins.

Colonial coinage Coinage of various colonies including Massachusetts Bay, New York, New Jersey, Rhode Island, Connecticut, Delaware, Maryland, Virginia, the Carolinas, and Georgia.

Commemorative A legal tender coin struck primarily for collectors.

Conjugate Two heads joined, as on the Eisenhower commemorative coin of 1990 depicting him both as soldier and as President.

Continental currency Coinage of 1776.

Cowrie shell A seashell used as a form of exchange.

Crane Paper Company For many years, the exclusive supplier of paper currency to the Bureau of Engraving & Printing.

Date The digits appearing on most coins to indicate the year a coin was made, though not always. Bicentennial coinage dated "1776–1976" was struck beginning in 1975.

Denarius Silver coin of ancient Rome, from about 211 B.C.; about 19 mm in size

Device Designs on a coin other than portraiture, such as mintmark, wildlife, scenery, etc.

Die The metal punch or device that is used to produce a coin on a press. The deeper the design is cut into the die, the higher the relief on the coin.

Die axis The way the dies are positioned in the coining press.

Dollar The currency unit of the United States of America. A truly international currency, as more than two-thirds of all U.S. $100 bills circulate abroad.

Double die When the image of the coin or its lettering appears to have been struck twice. Can be a doubly struck coin, or more likely a mistake in producing the die, doubling it, not the coin, which then mirrors the strike.

Eagle Denominational (U.S.). Depicted whole on the $10 gold piece, and divided on other coins: quarter eagle for $2.50, half eagle for $5, and double eagle $20. The bird on the reverse of the quarter, half and dollar of currently struck coins by act of Congress. Also appears on modern U.S. gold and silver bullion coins.

Edge The outside rim of a coin; its third side after obverse and reverse.

Edge lettering Lettering incused, engraved, or struck on a coin's third side.

Effigy Portrait that usually appears on the obverse of a coin. Can be singular or jugate (i.e., two portraits conjoined) such as the Eisenhower 1990 commemorative showing him both as a general and as President.

Error A coin or other numismatic item on which a mistake has been made.

Euro The currency system of the European Economic Union involving many countries and many designs.

Exergue The place on a coin or medal, usually below the central design, often giving the date of issue.

Exonumia Word coined (so to speak) by Russell Rulau to mean tokens and/or medals.

Field That portion not covered with the principal design on obverse and reverse.

Fineness The ratio, in a precious metal coin, that the precious metal bears to the whole. Most U.S. coins are .900 fine silver and gold. British sovereigns are .9167 fine.

Flan The metal disc—technically known by collectors as *planchet*—imprinted with the coin design.

Fort Knox The U.S. bullion depository built in 1937 to house gold reserves and now, ten 1933 double eagles.

Good A poor-condition circulated coin. (Yes, the concept is confusing.)

Groat British silver coin in circulation from 1279 to about 1955 (value 4 pence).

Half cent The smallest denomination struck by the U.S. Mint, produced from 1793 to 1857.

Hallmark A symbol of fineness and of manufacture.

Hub A piece of metal the exact size of the coin bearing the coin's design, cut by a janvier engraving machine, heat treated to harden it, then sharpened and improved by an engraver. It is then placed in a hydraulic press and slowly pressed into a blank piece of soft die steel until a negative replica is made (master die).

Incused design A design recessed into the coin's surface.

Ingot A square or rectangular-shaped metal mold, typically with its weight and fineness stamped thereon, into which bullion is poured.

Initials Usually of the engraver or sculptor who designed the coin and reproduced it in die form; for example, on the cent "VDB" are the initials of Victor David Brenner.

Inscription Verbiage appearing on coins either because it is required by law (statutory inscriptions) or because it is customarily used. "Liberty" is a statutory inscription on American coinage. The declamations of gratitude that appear on ancient Roman coins are the other kind.

Janvier engraver A transfer engraving machine which cuts the design into soft tool steel, tracing the exact details of the epoxy model and producing a positive replica of the model (a "hub") which is used to make dies.

Krugerrand South African gold bullion coin

Legal tender A coin or money that can be used for all debts, public or private, under legal compulsion.

Legend The inscription surrounding the effigy on a coin, typically of a monarch or emperor. For example, DEI GRA ("by the grace of God") appears in part on many British coins.

Maple Leaf Canadian bullion coin

Maria Theresa Thaler A trade coin made in 1780 by the Austro-Hungarian empire, and still minted today.

Medal A commemorative that is not a coin; generally larger in size.

Melting The common method for destroying coins. Coins are destroyed for many reasons, including that the metal they are made from is worth substantially more than their face value. Millions of gold and silver coins were destroyed this way when bullion prices rose above nominal value.

Metal composition How a struck coin appears: as clad-coinage (the U.S. quarter dollar), as one metal plated with another (the cent), solid gold (a 24 karat bullion coin) and otherwise.

Millimeters Metric measure used for coin size. The cent is 19 mm in diameter, the Morgan silver dollar 38.1 mm.

Mint Where coins are made; for example, Philadelpia, Denver, San Francisco, and West Point mints; the Casa de Moneda of Mexico; the Fabrica de la Moneda y Timbre in Madrid; La Zecca in Rome.

Mint set Uncirculated coins in a set made by the Mint and sold to collectors. In 1970, the "D" half dollar was included in mint sets but never for general circulation.

Mintage Number of pieces coined.

Mintmark A symbol appearing on coins to indicate the place they were produced, such as "D" for the Denver Mint.

Motto Phrases appearing on coinage such as "In God We Trust" or "E Pluribus Unum."

MS-65 An uncirculated coin of gem quality. MS-60 marks the start of uncirculated; from MS-65 to MS-70 is incremental perfection.

National motto For the United States, "In God We Trust."

NGC Numismatic Guaranty Corp. A commercial authentication and grading service which, for a fee, will tell you if your coin is genuine and rate its condition.

Nickel The 5 cent piece whose composition is 75 percent copper, 25 percent nickel. First used for coinage on the 5 cent piece in 1866.

No motto Coins struck in U.S. without the motto "In God We Trust." Among these are the 1907 $20 gold piece (restored by Act of Congress), the unique 1866 no motto quarter, and others.

Numismatic products Coins and coin-related products produced by or for the United States Mint for sale to the public.

Obverse The front or face of the coin. Typically bears the highest relief.

Olive branches Symbol of peace, found in the talons of the eagle on U.S. and other coinage.

Onza Mexican bullion coin.

Panda Chinese bullion coin.

Pattern coins Patterson DuBois noted in an early article that pattern or sample production ideas or issues are "half-forgotten witnesses . . . [to] the impractical schemes of visionaries and hobbyists."

PCGS Professional Coin Grading Service. A commercial authentication and grading service which, for a fee, will tell you if your coin is genuine and rate its condition.

Penny Colloquially, an American cent. A British coin from the eighth to fourteenth centuries, and in modern times, throughout the Commonwealth.

Planchet A blank metal flan that can be transformed into a coin. Collectible in its own right as a type I error (without rim) and type II (with upset rim).

Platinum Chemically described as a the 78th element on the periodic table with a high density of 21.5 grams per cubic centimeter, and a melting point of 3,224 degrees Fahrenheit, platinum is also the most valuable "impurity" of most nickel deposits. The mining of nickel is where the platinum group of metals—ruthenium, palladium, osmium, and iridium—come from. Discovered by Italian scientist Julius Scaliger in 1557, large quantities of the metal were not available until about 1750, when the Spaniards found it in Peru. They named it platinum from their word "plata," which is Spanish for silver.

Precious metal Generally refers to coining metals of gold, silver, and platinum.

Presidential dollar Coin series starting in 2007

honoring the nation's (deceased) former chief executives.

Privy mark Indicates who was the mintmaster in charge when coins were produced.

Proof A coin struck primarily for collectors on a highly polished planchet using highly polished dies, usually on a hydraulic press, and sometimes more than once to bring up the relief. The specially treated die produces a mirrored background, sharp relief, and a frosted image on the finished coin.

Proof set Proof coins sold by the Mint to collectors going back to the 1860s, but since 1936 packaged and marketed by the Mint.

Regulation An administrative rule made by a governmental department, frequently based on laws. For coin matters, usually administered by the Treasury Department.

Restrike A numismatic item that is reproduced, sometimes using original dies, sometimes with new dies made from an original hub, usually for collectors. The 1827 quarter and 1804 silver dollar are two examples of highly collectible restrikes.

Reverse The back of the coin with a lower relief than the obverse.

Rim The edge of a coin. On the dollar, the "In God We Trust" motto is currently inscribed on the rim.

Sacagawea dollar Golden dollar (manganese/brass composition), struck since 2000, honoring the guide to explorers Lewis and Clark.

Saint-Gaudens Augustus Saint-Gaudens, the great American sculptor and designer of the $10 and $20 gold pieces struck 1907 to 1933. The double eagles are universally referred to as "Saints" if they bear his magnificent design.

Screw press Before coining presses were automated,

the coining press operated on a giant screw and moved up and down, applying pressure to produce the coin.

Scrip A "near money" that is not legal tender but allows people to redeem for goods or trade.

Secondary device Appears on a coin as not the primary design from a focal point of view.

Silver dollar A dollar type struck from 1794 to 1935 and again from 1971 to 1978, but commonly used as a generic term for the dollar coin.

State coinage Coinage of twelve of the thirteen original colonies, used between 1776 and 1789.

State quarters The quarter dollars produced at the direction of Congress, starting in 1999, honoring all fifty American states.

Statutory inscriptions Mottoes or verbiage that appear on a coin because the law so requires.

Stella U.S. $4 gold piece pattern, 1879 to 1880.

Sterling In silver, .925 fine, typical of the British pound sterling.

Surcharge An amount added to the selling price of a commemorative coin. The surcharge amount and the beneficiary organizations are specified in the commemorative coin legislation.

TAMS Token & Medal Society, a group of exonumists.

Tetradrachm Ancient Greek coin with a value of four drachma.

Token A non-legal tender object similar to a coin that can be used for buying goods or services. Can be made of metal, cardboard, or virtually any media.

Trade coin A coin not necessarily legal tender whose design, weight and purity is intended to be a bullion substitute. The U.S. Trade dollar (1873–1885) is one example; the Maria Theresa Thaler (all dated 1780) is another.

Trial of the Pyx From an ancient English term describing a group of citizens (the Assay Commission) appointed by the U.S. President, who examines and melts coins for proper weight. The annual Assay Commission was authorized and directed by the original Mint Act of April 2, 1792, and continued uninterrupted until 1980 when it was finally abolished. Designed to maintain oversight over a narrow aspect of the executive branch, it examined the nation's coins on an annual basis and certified to the President, Congress, and the American people that gold and silver coins had the necessary purity, the proper weight, and necessarily, value.

Trimes Three-cent pieces. Struck in silver (1851–1873). During World War II, they were authorized again, and called "Paddies."

Troy weight The weight of gold or silver in a coin (twelve ounces to the pound) calculated by taking gross weight and multiplying by fineness.

Uncirculated A coin, usually in brilliant, shiny condition, that has not yet entered general circulation. Uncirculated coins have a satin finish versus the mirrored background and frosted image of proof coins.

Upsetting The creation of a rim or edge on a coin—its third side—when the blanks go through an upsetting mill.

Wampum Beads made from conch shells, used as a medium of exchange well into the nineteeth century.

Weight The gross weight of a coin, usually given in grains or grams.

SELECTED BIBLIOGRAPHY

Akers, David W., *United States Double Eagles 1849–1933* (1982).

Akers, David W., *United States Eagles 1795–1933* (1980).

Akers, David W., *United States Gold Dollars 1849–1889 (1975).*

Akers, David W., *United States Half Eagles 1795–1929* (1979).

Akers, David W., *United States Quarter Eagles 1796–1929* (1975).

Akers, David W., *United States Three Dollar Gold Pieces* (1976).

Bagg & Jelinski, "Trends in Grading: A Review of the Literature," 89 *The Numismatist* 2661 (1976).

Berman, Neil S., and Hans M.F. Schulman, *The Investor's Guide to United States Coins* (1986).

Berman, Neil S. and DiGenova, Silvano. *The Investor's Guide to United States Coins: A Complete Statistical Analysis of How Coin Collectors Profit With Rare Coins* (2007).

Bowers, Q. David, *A Guidebook of Shield and Liberty Head Nickels: Complete Source for History, Grading, and Prices* (2006).

Bowers, Q. David, *Adventures With Rare Coins* (1979).

Bowers, Q. David, *Common Sense Coin Investment* (1982).

Bowers, Q. David, *Guidebook of Double Eagle Gold Coins: A Complete History And Price Guide* (2004).

Bowers, Q. David, *Guidebook of Morgan Silver Dollars, a Complete History and Price Guide* (2005).

Bowers, Q. David, *Guidebook of United States Type Coins* (2005).

Bowers, Q. David, "Numismatic Nostalgia: ANACS Grading Policies Amended," 95 *The Numismatist* 2510 (1982).

Bowers, Q. David, *The Expert's Guide to Collecting and Investing in Rare Coins: Secrets of Success Coins, Tokens, Medals, Paper Money* (2005).

Bowers, Q. David, *The History of United States Coins as Illustrated by the Garrett Collection* (1979).

Bowers, Q. David, *The Official Red Book of Morgan Silver Dollars, 1878 to 1921* (2004).

Bowers, Q. David, *United States Gold Coins: An Illustrated History* (1982).

Bressett, Ken E., *Basics of Coin Grading for United States Coins* (1982).

Bressett, Ken E., and A. Kosoff, eds., *Official A.N.A. Grading Standards for United States Coins* (3d ed., 1987).

Bressett, Kenneth (ed.) *The Official American Numismatic Association Grading Standards for United States Coins* (6th ed., 2005).

Brown, Martin. R., and John W. Dunn, *A Guide to the Grading of United States Coins* (6th ed., 1975).

Carlton, R. Scott, *The International Encyclopedic Dictionary of Numismatics* (1996).

Coin World Almanac (6th ed., 1990).

Numismatist 1194 (1981).

Doty, Richard, *Coins of the World* (1978).

Doty, Richard, *The Macmillan Encyclopedic Dictionary of Numismatics* (1982).

Fivaz, Bill, "Developing Grading Skills," 95 *The Numismatist* 1715 (1982).

Fivaz, Bill, *United States Gold Counterfeit Detection Guide* (2005).

Friedberg, A., *Gold Coins of the World* (5th ed., 1980).

Frey, Albert, *Dictionary of Numismatic Names* (1917).

Friedberg, Arthur and Ira., *Paper Money of the United States* (18th ed 2006).

Friedberg, A., *Guidebook of United States Paper Money* (2005).

Friedberg, Arthur & Ira., *Gold Coins of the World From Ancient Times to the Present* (7th Edition, 2003).

Ganz, David L., "14 Bits: A Legal and Legislative History of 31 U.S.C. §§324d-324i" (1976).

Ganz, David L., *Planning Your Rare Coin Retirement* (1998).

Ganz, David L., *Proof of Value of Coin Collection, 95 Proof of Facts* 3d 155–465 (2007).

Ganz, David L., *The Official Guide to Americas State Quarters* (rev. ed., 2000) and manuscript for 2008 2nd edition.

Ganz, David L., *The Official Guide to Commemorative Coins* (1999).

Ganz, David L., *The World of Coins and Coin Collecting* (3d ed., 1998).

Ganz, David L., "Toward a Revision of the Minting and Coinage Laws of the United States," 26 *Cleveland State Law Review* 175–257 (1977).

Ganz, David L., "Value of coin collection, 5 Proof of Facts 3d 577" (1989).

Levinson, Robert, *The Standard Catalog of Dated European Coins from 1234–1500: An Illustrated Catalogue and Guide to Dated Medieval Coins* (2007).

Mudd, Douglas, *All the Money in the World* (2006).

Opitz, Charles J., *An Ethnographic Study of Traditional Money* (2000).

Quiggin, A. H., *A Survey of Primitive Money* (Spink reprint, 1978).

Raymond, W., *Standard Catalogue of United States Coins* (1935–1957, annual issues).

Reed, M., *Encyclopedia of U.S. Coins* (2d ed., 1972).

Ruddy, James F., *New Photograde: A Photographic Grading Guide for United States Coins* (1970, 11th printing, 1979).

Selim, Robert & Douglas Mudd, Smithsonian Institution. National Museum of American History. *Parthia: The Forgotten Empire: A Virtual Exhibition* / Smithsonian Institution. National Museum of American History. (2000).

Sheldon, William. H., *Penny Whimsy* (1958) (a revision of *Early American Cents 1793–1814 (1949))*.

Taglione, Paul. F., *A Reference to United States Federal Gold Coinage* (multiple volumes, 1986 to present).

Taxay, Don, *The U.S. Mint and Coinage* (1966).

Travers, Scott A., *The Coin Collector's Survival Manual* (rev. 4th ed. 2003).

Travers, Scott A., ed., *Official Guide to Coin Grading & Counterfeit Detection* (1997).

Travers, Scott A., *The Insider's Guide to U.S. Coin Values 2007*.

Yeoman, R. S., *A Catalogue of Modern World Coin* (13th ed., 1984).

Yeoman, R. S., *Current Coins of the World* (8th ed. 1988).

Yeoman, R. S., *A Guide Book of United States Coins* (35th ed., 1982) (annual editions, 1947 to date)(60th ed., 2007).

Yeoman, R. S., *Handbook of United States Coins* (64th ed., 2007).

ACKNOWLEDGMENTS

Those who are acknowledged have worked with me on many projects over the years. They are friends, colleagues, professional numismatists, or closely associated with the field. When I started college at Georgetown University's School of Foreign Service in 1969, I also became the Washington Correspondent for Numismatic News Weekly, the oldest hobby periodical. I started making my rounds to congressional offices, the U.S. Mint, the Bureau of Engraving and Printing, and other numismatic areas of the nation's capital. It wasn't long before I had an appointment to see Dr. Vladimir ("Doc") Clain-Stefanelli and Elvira ("Lisa") Clain-Stefanelli, his wife.

Doc and Lisa were the husband and wife curators of the Smithsonian Institution's National Numismatic Collection. Each was devoted to each other and to the National Numismatic Collection. Over the years, I participated in many events and symposiums sponsored at the national numismatic collection. Each December, I would call and ask Doc or Lisa if a piece or two from my own collection would be useful as a donation to the National Numismatic Collection—and so it is that a 1974 aluminum cent planchet blank is there together with some other choice morsels that Mrs. Stefanelli, particularly, persuaded me belonged to the people of the United States rather than in my own collection.

Doc and Lisa were powerful persuaders who built and lovingly sustained the collection.

I got to know Lisa much better when we both served as charter members of the Citizens Commemorative Coin Advisory Committee during the Clinton administration, and it was during a special tour of the coin cabinet for that committee that I received a behind-the-scenes look at the real treasures of the Smithsonian, which was perhaps the genesis of this book.

Since 1973, I have been a contributing editor to *COINage Magazine*, and in May of 2006, Marcy Gibbel, its managing editor, sent a note from Karen Jones of the Band-F group to her stable of writers, seeking an author to write this book. I sent some clips and a resume, and before long spoke with Karen and her partner with the most unlikely of monikers, F-Stop Fitzgerald. From another hobby, I immediately recognized "F-Stop" as a true photographer.

F-Stop and Karen cajoled an outline and gave me a solid deadline. They also found a first-rate production coordinator in Mie Kingsley, and a first-rate editor in Diane Patrick, who asked questions thoughtfully, parsed words with a lance, and always let me find my own voice rather than inserting her own. I know I was difficult to work with, and I apologize; you have made this book better.

Photos for coin books are always difficult, but they are essential to the successful presentation of any numismatic story. Credit for the success of the photos in this book really goes to Jim Halperin and Steve Ivy, the co-chairmen of Heritage Auction Galleries, whose www.ha.com website made for one-stop shopping, and whose photo department was of immeasurable assistance. Jim Halperin has lent this type of a hand to me for more than a quarter century, and I am much obliged. The graciousness with which he has offered his firm's excellent library of numismatic items for illustration was indispensable to the timely completion of the project. The responsibility for providing the photos fell on Cathy Hadd and Kelley Norwine, who have my gratitude and thanks.

Thanks, also, to several professional numismatists who graciously consented to allow their photos to be used in this book: Steve Rubinger of Numisma, Alan Davisson, and Ira and Lawrence Goldberg, who have never turned down a request in the more than 30 years we have known each other. It is also only fitting that the Goldberg cousins be given their due for selling the world's first $100,000 coin in 1973.

Kudos, too, to Teletrade, the online auction house, whose excellent website helped in the valuation of coins as well as the location of several otherwise hard-to-find photos. Their consent to the use of their photos is deeply appreciated.

Ken Potter supplied some otherwise impossible-to-find error photos.

Thanks, too, to the Smithsonian Institution National Numismatic Collection, and especially my good friend Dr. Richard Doty, who I have known since he was a curator of the American Numismatic Society. He read the manuscript and made valuable suggestions.

The graciousness of the American Numismatic Society in New York, of which I am one of 200 life fellows, is significant and appreciated. Their assistance with ancient coin photos from the Robert F. Kelley collection, along with other rarities, is appreciated, and reminds me of how the circle is round. In the late 1970s, while an ANS associate member and a member of the Board of Directors of the Georgetown University Library, I stumbled on the numismatic papers of the late Robert Kelley and persuaded University Librarian Joseph Jeffs that they belonged with the Kelley coins at the ANS; they were of use in preparing portions of this manuscript, and I thank the Lauinger Library at Georgetown for its assistance in obtaining the data many years ago. The online ANS Library was also enormously helpful.

The collection of the late Harry Bass (on display online and at the Edward C. Rochette Money Museum of the American Numismatic Association in Colorado Springs), and the Eric P. Newman Money Museum (on the campus of Washington University at St. Louis), are two additional resources that were used in the preparation of this volume. Special thanks to John Nebel for allowing his photography to be used and to Eric and Evelyn Newman for opening the doors of the Newman Money Museum to me and this book project. David Calhoun of the Bass Foundation and Doris

Bass, Harry's widow and keeper of the light, are specifically thanked for allowing the Nebel photo to be used; it is one of the finest museum photos I've ever seen.

Many of the error coins that were photographed for this book came from my own collection; Fred Weinberg (www.FredWeinberg.com) has been a consistent and good source for these mint errors, and a good friend of many years' duration. Without his indulgence, the choice of photos would be the poorer. Also of great assistance in gathering error photos was Ken Potter, whose graciousness under my time pressures is deeply appreciated.

Thanks as well to Whitman Publishing (Dennis Tucker, president) and Littleton Coin Company (David Sundman, president) for help in obtaining photos of hobby supplies.

Also appreciated is the assistance of the American Numismatic Association, the national coin club (I served as forty-eighth President from 1993–1995), whose online library and photographic services helped this book immeasurably. I have a fondness for the ANA; it is there that I met my wife Kathy Gotsch, who is thanked for bolstering both the author and the book. Thanks to its executive director, Chris Cipoletti.

This book was written over a six month period and could not have been completed without Kathy. It took me from her on too many evenings, weekends, and other times, including a recent 5,000-mile cruise from Dubai to Istanbul. Thanks again for making this a better book, and for sharing my passion.

That cruise, and an earlier one to Antarctica—and in fact many of the foreign sidebar stories—was made possible by my dear friend of nearly forty years, Paul R. Whitnah, a principal of M & M Travel in Arlington (suburban Dallas-Fort Worth) Texas, who has handled Kathy's and my travel for many years despite the 1,200-mile distance from his office to mine. He has always let me know the numismatic components of a trip, and shared my travelogues and friendship.

Finally, I confess to having two secret lives. One is as a lawyer—senior partner in the New York City law firm of Ganz & Hollinger P.C., and the Fair Lawn, New Jersey firm of Ganz & Sivin, LLP. My partners of more than twenty-five years, Jeri Hollinger and Teri Towe, are thanked for their understanding of this "numismatic thing" that I do, and my secretary, Iyesha Jones, and administrative assistant, Rekha Sharma, who got involved in correspondence and tracking down last-minute fact checking. The other is as a member of the Board of Chosen Freeholders of Bergen County, a sort of county supervisor in a legislative capacity, where I have served as budget chair for the past five years. I thank my colleagues for their patience in the final rush for this manuscript as it competed with the people's business, and I thank my legislative aide, Jennifer Rachaner, for being so cheerful and doing the needed legislative research that freed me up to complete this book on time.

I am certain that I have forgotten some who assisted in making this book come alive. It is not intentional. And despite the help, which has made it a better book, the mistakes I acknowledge are my own.

—David L. Ganz

PHOTO CREDITS

OPPOSITE: 2007 Presidential $1 coin commemorating the first president of the United States.

Page 4, bottom; Page 87, bottom right; Page 98, top left; Page 99, bottom right; Page 132, middle; Page 133, bottom; Page 137, bottom; courtesy of Smithsonian Institution National Coin Collection

Page 84; Page 88, bottom right; courtesy of Teletrade

TOC (pages v, vi), all images; Page 2, top; Page 2, bottom; Page 7, bottom; Page 34, bottom; Page 42, all images; Page 43, bottom; Page 44, top; Page 45, bottom; Page 46, bottom; Page 47, top; Page 50, top; Page 51, top left; Page 57, bottom; Page 60, all images; Page 78, bottom left; Page 128; Page 130, bottom; Page 152; courtesy of the U.S. Mint

Page 74, bottom; Page 75, bottom; courtesy of Whitman Publishing

Page 6, top; courtesy of World Wide Coin Investments

Many of the photographs throughout this book were made available through the generosity of Heritage Auction Galleries, whose photographers are known for taking some of the finest coin shots. This heavily illustrated book would not have been possible without their assistance and that of their staff. Readers interested in seeing enlarged examples of any of their coins are invited to go to the company's extensive web site, www.HA.com, and use the viewer to see the coins up close.

Page 3, bottom; Page 4, top; Page 5, bottom; Page 8; Page 10, top; Page 12, all images; Page 13, all images; Page 14, bottom; Page 15, all images; Page 17, top; Page 18, bottom; Page 20; Page 22 all images; Page 23, all images; Page 25, all images; Page 27, top; Page 28, all images; Page 29, all images; Page 30, all images; Page 32, bottom; Page 33, all images; Page 34, top; Page 35, top; Page 37, all images; Page 39, all images; Page 40, bottom; Page 50, bottom; Page 51, top right; Page 51, bottom; Page 52, all images; Page 53, top; Page 55, top; Page 57, top; Page 61, bottom right; Page 62, all images; Page 63, all images; Page 64, top; Page 65, all images; Page 67, all images; Page 69, all images; Page 79, all images; Page 80, bottom; Page 81, top; Page 83, top; Page 87, top left; Page 87, bottom left; Page 88, bottom left; Page 89, top; Page 89, bottom left; Page 93, top; Page 95, top; Page 96; Page 98, top right; Page 98, bottom; Page 99, top; Page 99, bottom left; Page 100, all images; Page 101, top; Page 102, top; Page 103, top; Page 105, bottom; Page 106, all images; Page 107, top; Page 109, top; Page 110, all images; Page 111, top; Page 112; Page 114, all images; Page 115, all images; Page 116, all images; Page 118, all images; Page 122, bottom; Page 123, top; Page 127, bottom; Page 136, top; Page 137, top; Page 138, bottom; Page 139, top; Page 140, all images; courtesy of Heritage Auction Galleries